Calgary LRT Walks:
The Northwest Stations

Thirty-Six Walks - Nine Stations

David Peyto

David Peyto [signature]

Peyto Lake Books

Published by Peyto Lake Books, Calgary, AB.
Email info@peytolakebooks.com
Website www.peytolakebooks.com

Printed and bound in Canada by Blitzprint, Calgary

Copyright 2013 by David Peyto

Library and Archives Canada Cataloguing in Publication

Peyto, David W., author
    Calgary LRT walks : the northwest stations / David Peyto.

"Thirty-six walks—nine stations".
Includes bibliographical references.
ISBN 978-0-9919150-0-2 (pbk.)

    1. Roads—Alberta—Calgary—Guidebooks.
2. Street-railroad stations—Alberta—Calgary—Guidebooks.
3. Calgary (Alta.)—Guidebooks. I. Title.

FC3697.67.P49 2013   917.123'38   C2013-902207-4

The front cover photos are King George School at 20th Avenue and 10th Street NW and the Bow River Pathway west of Home Road NW.
The back cover photo is Research Park at 40th Avenue & 37th Street NW
All photos in the book unless otherwise indicated were taken by the author.

Dedication
This book is dedicated to Emma, a future hiker.

Acknowledgements

It takes more than one person to create and publish a book. This book is no exception. I am fortunate to have the support of several people.

I want to thank my wife, Linda. As I developed the outline of this book I appreciated being able to share my ideas with her.

From the time I self-published my first book in 2002, my sisters, Margaret Peyto and Carol Cole, have been a tremendous support, taking the time to proof read the text for all my books and to provide me with positive suggestions.

Thank you to my brother-in-law, Ron Cole, and my nephews, Andrew, Ethan and Tim Cole, and my niece, Yolande Cole, for their support during the writing of my books.

Thank you to Blitzprint for their assistance with printing my books.

Thank you to Calgary Transit for their interest in this book.

Thank you to Glenbow Museum Archives for permission to use the historic photos in this book.

My decision to organize and write this type of walking guidebook was made after reading *Sky Train Explorer* by John Atkin. His book describes heritage walks from every station between Vancouver's Waterfront Station and the New Westminster Station.

Disclaimer

This book is a guide and should be used as such. Route conditions may change due to weather, lack of path or trail maintenance or other factors. *Calgary LRT Walks: The Northwest Stations* reports conditions along each route at the time of writing but does not recommend whether or not you should go on each walk. It is necessary to plan ahead based on your ability and the weather. The author and publisher is not responsible for any loss, damage, expense, injury or any other liability whatsoever suffered by any person resulting directly or indirectly from using this guidebook. Please be aware that you are walking at your own risk.

Contents

Introduction

Calgary LRT Walks: The Northwest Stations provides information about thirty-six walks that start and/or finish at one of the nine Northwest Stations. The chapters are arranged in the same sequence as the stations if you ride the train from downtown to the end of the Northwest line. These stations are Sunnyside, SAIT/ACAD/Jubilee, Lions Park, Banff Trail, University, Brentwood, Dalhousie, Crowfoot and Tuscany. At the time of writing the Tuscany Station is still under construction with the scheduled opening of the station set for 2014. In the text temporary bus route instructions are included to get you to the start of the Tuscany walks from the Crowfoot Station. When the Tuscany Station opens you can then ignore these bus route instructions.

This book is one of a series of Calgary LRT Walks books. *Calgary LRT Walks: The South Stations* provides information about thirty-eight walks that start and/or finish at one of the eleven South Stations. I am currently researching routes for additional books in this series. I hope the *Calgary LRT Walks* books will encourage readers to explore Calgary in a unique way. Thinking about the environment, you might leave your vehicle at home and take a bus to the nearest station.

Enjoy yourself as you head out on your explorations. You will have the opportunity to discover many facets of Calgary, walking past historic buildings in older communities, viewing works of art, visiting old and new parks and green spaces, stopping at viewpoints, exploring trails and wandering the sidewalks and pathways in some of Calgary's newer communities. You may want to walk more than one shorter route on the same day.

Each walk is written in a similar format. To assist the reader in deciding the walk to select there are brief notes for each route under the following headings.

Station Information: Each chapter begins with a physical description of the station and information about buildings and communities adjacent to the station.

Walk Overview: This section provides a description of the area in which the walk is located, noting some of the more interesting locations along the route. These locations may include riverside pathways, natural areas, viewpoints, community parks or historic buildings. The walk may be a loop route, an out-and-back route, a linear route or a combination of these options. If a walk is in an isolated area this is mentioned in the text.

Length: This refers to the approximate distance for the walk (in kilometres).

Route Description & Accessibility: Information is provided about the accessibility of each route for users of wheelchairs or baby strollers. This description includes the type of walking surface – paved, sidewalks, gravel, dirt or grass. The level of difficulty (flat or gently rolling, small hills or steep ascents or descents) is also mentioned. On some walks an alternate route or detour with better accessibility is included in the text.

Food and Drink: Information is provided about parks, green spaces and viewpoints along or near the route where you can stop and enjoy your drink and lunch or snack. Information is also provided about coffee shops, grocery stores, convenience stores and restaurants located along or near the route.

Washrooms: This section lists the locations of washrooms in parks or public buildings along the route. Please remember that the washrooms in restaurants, coffee shops or stores are for customers only. Some washrooms in parks are seasonal and are only open from the Victoria Day long weekend in May to the Thanksgiving long weekend in October.

Map References: Map page numbers for each walk are given using the following four map books as references. Walkers are encouraged to take the map book of their choice, or a Calgary Transit Map, or a Calgary Pathways and Bikeways Map and this guidebook on each walk. Calgary Transit Maps and Calgary Pathway and Bikeways Maps are available at any Calgary Public Library.

- Clearview – Clearview Map of Calgary 2011 Edition
- MapArt – MapArt Calgary & Southern Alberta – Large Print 2011 Edition
- Rand McNally – Rand McNally Calgary 2008 Edition
- Sherlock – Sherlock's Map of Calgary 14th Edition 2012

Route Category: The routes have been divided into four categories.

Walk: This type of route starts and finishes at the station. The walk may be a loop, an out-and-back or a combination of both. There are twenty-two Northwest Stations walks in this category.

Sunnyside Walks 1, 2, 3, 4, 5
SAIT/ACAD/Jubilee Walks 1, 2, 3
Lions Park Walks 1, 3
Banff Trail Walks 1,2
University Walks 1, 2
Brentwood Walks 1, 3
Dalhousie Walks 4, 5
Tuscany Walks 1, 2, 3, 4

Bus/Walk: This type of route involves riding a bus from the station to the starting point of the walk. The walking route is then a linear walk ending back at the station. There are two Northwest Stations walks in this category.
Dalhousie Walk 1

Crowfoot Walk 1

Walk/Bus: This type of route starts from the station and after a linear walking route there is a bus ride back to the station from the finishing point of the walk. Only one Northwest Station walk is in this category.

Crowfoot Walk 2

Bus/Walk/Bus: This type of route involves riding a bus from the station to the starting point of the walk. The walk might be a loop, an out-and-back, a linear or a combination. At the end of the walk there is a bus ride from the finish back to the station. There are ten Northwest Stations walks in this category.

Sunnyside Walk 6

Lions Park Walk 2

Brentwood Walk 2

Dalhousie Walks 2, 3, 6, 7, 8

Crowfoot Walks 3, 4

Bus Directions from the station to the start of the walk: This section includes the four-digit bus stop number at the station and the four-digit bus stop number and its location at the start of the walk. The scheduled time for the bus to travel from the station stop to the stop at the start of the route and the frequency of service for that route during mid-day (8:30 am to 4:00 pm) on weekdays and on Saturdays and Sundays is also included.

The Walk: This section describes the route in detail. In the text I have used the following terms. *Path* refers to any paved path or pathway. *Trail* includes any dirt, cinder or gravel surfaces. *Gateway* is used in the text to indicate an opening in a fence.

Bus Directions from the end of the walk to the station: This section includes the four-digit bus stop number and location for the bus stop at the end of the walk and the four-digit bus stop number for the stop at the station. The scheduled time for the bus to travel from the stop at the end of the walk to the stop back at the station and the frequency of service for that route during mid-day (8:30 am to 4:00 pm) on weekdays and on Saturdays and Sundays is also included.

Route Summary: This section at the end of each walk summarizes the route directions.

What to take

The following items are recommended:
- A good pair of walking shoes or boots
- Clothing and a hat suitable for Calgary's very changeable weather

- Water or juice and lunch or a snack
- Train/bus fare money, a transit timetable and a Calgary Transit map
- A city map of your choice and this guidebook
- Sunscreen and/or insect repellent depending on the time of year
- A first-aid kit containing bandages, moleskin, tape, antiseptic ointment and a pair of folding scissors
- A camera and books about birds or flowers are optional
- Sunglasses
- A compass
- A backpack to carry everything

Transit Fares

At the time of writing an adult single fare is $3.00 and a youth single fare (6 to 14) is $1.75. Children under 6 ride for free. You can also purchase books of ten tickets ($30.00 for adults and $17.50 for youth). A day pass is $9.00 for adults and $5.75 for youth. A monthly pass costs $94 for adults and $57.50 for youth. Seniors over 65 can purchase a yearly pass for $94 beginning July 1st, 2013. The Calgary Transit website lists the fare vendors. The city-wide vendors include Calgary Co-op, Canada Safeway, Mac's Convenience Stores and 7-Eleven Food Stores. The downtown vendors include the Calgary Transit Customer Service Centre at 224 – 7th Avenue SE and City Hall Cashiers.

Calgary Transit Customer Service

The Calgary Transit website is www.calgarytransit.com
The Calgary Transit Call Centre phone number is 403-262-1000. The Transit Call Centre hours are 6 am to 9 pm on weekdays and 8 am to 6 pm on weekends and some holidays. Call for information on routes, schedules, fares and other services or let the Centre know if you have a commendation, suggestion, or concern about any of Calgary Transit's services.
The Teletype Number (TTY) for hearing impaired customers is 403-268-8087.
The Customer Service Centre at 224 – 7th Avenue SW is open weekdays only from 10 am to 5:30 pm. Obtain passes, tickets, information, route maps, schedules or pick up lost property at the Customer Service Centre. Lost property phone inquiries can be made at 403-268-1600 on weekdays from 10 am to 5:30 pm.

The Access Calgary phone number 403-537-7770 is for inquiries about Access Calgary services.

How to Use Teleride

It is easy to connect with your Teleride bus stop numbers. Go to the bus stop that you use and record the four-digit Teleride bus stop number for your route. Call the Teleride phone number 403-974-4000 and enter your four-digit stop number. There are three types of information you can access to help you use Calgary Transit.

Press 1 to obtain current bus times (the next two or three buses). Call every day. Teleride tells you if there are any delays on your route caused by detours, construction, weather or traffic.

Press 2 to obtain future bus times (buses you want at a later date or time, up to a week in advance).

Press 3 to obtain general transit information on fares, special events, etc.

All four-digit stop numbers for the station bus stops and the stops at the start and finish of walks are included in the text on the walks that require a bus.

Calgary Transit History

The Calgary Municipal Railway

The Calgary Municipal Railway (CMR) provided streetcar service to Calgarians from 1909 to 1950, a time that included World War I and II and the Great Depression of the 1930s. The CMR also operated Bowness Park.

Calgary Transit System

From 1947 to 1950 the newly-named Calgary Transit System began to phase out the use of streetcars combined with the introduction of electrically-powered trolley coaches. Gasoline and diesel-powered buses also began operating. On June 1st, 1947, the first trolley coach operated on the Crescent Heights route. On December 29th, 1950, the last streetcar travelled on the Ogden route. In 1970 the Calgary Transit System was renamed Calgary Transit. The trolley coaches stopped operating on March 8th, 1975.

LRT History

Route 201 (Red Line) presently operates from Crowfoot Station on the Northwest line to Somerset-Bridlewood Station on the South line. In 1979 construction began on a 12.5 km light rail transit line from 8th Street West downtown south to Anderson Road. The LRT made its inaugural run on this line on May 25th, 1981. In 1987 the Northwest line began operating from

11

the University Station to Downtown. Three years later the Northwest line was extended to Brentwood Station. The South line was then extended two more stations to Canyon Meadows and Fish Creek-Lacombe Stations in 2001. In 2003 the Northwest line was extended one more station to Dalhousie Station. Another two stations were added to the South line in 2004 as the line was extended to Shawnessy and Somerset-Bridlewood Stations. Crowfoot Station on the Northwest line opened in June 2009. Tuscany Station is scheduled to open in 2014.

Route 202 (Blue Line) is from 69th Street Station on the West line to Saddletowne Station on the Northeast line. In 1985 the Northeast line began operating between Whitehorn Station and 8th Street West Station. McKnight-Westwinds Stations Station on the Northeast line opened in 2007. Martindale and Saddletowne Stations on the Northeast line opened in August 2012. The six stations on the West line opened in December 2012 as part of Route 202 (Blue Line). Future plans include a Southeast line and a North Central line.

Wading Pool at Riley Park

Chapter One
Sunnyside Station

Station Information: Sunnyside is the first station on the Northwest line after leaving the downtown 7th Street Station. The station is on the east side of 9A Street between 3rd and 4th Avenues. Stairs and ramps provide access for the two side-loading platforms. There are pedestrian crossings of the tracks at both ends of the platforms.

The community of Sunnyside is east of 10th Street between McHugh Bluff on the north side of the community and Memorial Drive on the south side of the community. Felix McHugh began homesteading in this area in 1883 having travelled west from Ottawa prior to the construction of the railway reaching Calgary. The area that he homesteaded was subdivided in 1906-07 and became Sunnyside. In 1990, McHugh Bluff, the 27 hectares of escarpment slope on the north side of the community, was named after McHugh.

Sunnyside began as a working class community. Today the community has evolved into a mixture of older houses, new infill houses, condos, townhouses, and walk-up apartment buildings. In the past the Bow River on the south side of the community would occasionally overflow its banks flooding Sunnyside. The construction of dikes along the north bank of the river has helped alleviate this problem.

The community of Hillhurst is west of 10th Street. Thomas Riley and his family settled in this area after they arrived in Calgary in 1887. Thomas' son, Ezra Riley, subdivided the property and began selling lots in 1904. In 1910 Ezra donated 8.1 hectares of land to the city for park use. Riley Park on the north side of the community is at the base of the escarpment that extends along the north side of Hillhurst. SAIT Polytechnic, the Alberta College of Art and Design and the Southern Alberta Jubilee Auditorium are all located at the top of this escarpment. Today Hillhurst is a mix of older houses, new infill houses and townhouses, some smaller walk-up apartment buildings and a few high-rise apartments on the edges of the district. The community was named for Hillhurst Farm at Compton, Quebec. Senator H.M. Cochrane, the founder of the Cochrane Ranche Company. came from Compton.

On 10th Street, the dividing line between the two communities, there are a variety of retail stores, coffee shops, restaurants and other assorted businesses. Kensington Road that runs in an east-west direction near the south side of Hillhurst has a similar assortment of businesses. There is also a commercial area on the west side of Hillhurst along 14th Street.

Sunnyside Walk One
Sunnyside – Long Loop

Walk Overview: This loop route roughly follows the outer edge of the Sunnyside community. The first half of the walk includes the Sunnyside Pathway along the lower edge of the McHugh Bluff escarpment slope. After strolling along Memorial Drive from 3rd Street to 10th Street, the walk heads north past the shops, coffee shops and restaurants of 10th Street on the way back to the station. Points of interest along the route include McHugh Bluff, several historic buildings and window-shopping along 10th Street.

Length: 3.5 km

Route Description & Accessibility: Most of this route is relatively flat with good accessibility. The exception is the Sunnyside Pathway along the lower edge of McHugh Bluff. This pathway has a short steep ascent followed by a more gradual descent. Information on a detour that avoids this section is included in the text. The walking surface along the route is a mix of sidewalks and paved paths.

Food and Drink: After the walk you could head for Riley Park north of 5th Avenue and west of 10th Street to relax at one of the tables or benches. There is a grocery store adjacent to the station. On 10th Street and Kensington Road there are several choices of restaurants and coffee shops.

Washrooms: Riley Park has seasonal public washrooms.

Map References: Clear-View – 28, MapArt – 154 & 164
Rand McNally – 49 & 50, Sherlock – 27

Route Category: Walk – The route starts and ends at the station (no bus is required).

The Walk: This route starts on the east side of the tracks at 4th Avenue. Passengers getting off the northbound Crowfoot train walk to the front end of the platform and descend a few steps to 4th Avenue. Passengers getting off the southbound Somerset-Bridlewood train walk to the back end of the platform, descend a few steps and turn right crossing both sets of tracks to the front end of the northbound platform.

Begin the walk heading northeasterly on 4th Avenue two blocks to 7th Street. At this corner you are across the street from the steep slopes near the west end of McHugh Bluff. A rather primitive trail can be seen climbing up the steep escarpment slope. On the east side of 7th Street the sidewalk stamp on the property line between the two older houses is dated 1913 and is inscribed as 4th Avenue. Turn right on 7th Street and walk one block south to 3rd Avenue. Make a left turn and continue in a northeasterly direction along the north side of 3rd Avenue. Just beyond 6th Street keep your eyes

Rocks enclosed in wire keep the slope
from sliding onto the Sunnyside Pathway

open for three gargoyles sitting in a tree on the south side of 3rd Avenue. These creative pieces of art add a delightful touch to this street. The row of houses along 3rd Avenue in the 600 block are a good example of the workers cottages constructed by the Canadian Pacific Railway and rented to their employees.

Your route turns to the left across the street from the gargoyles and follows the paved Sunnyside Pathway up through the trees at the base of the escarpment (0.6 km). The discovery of bones in this area indicates that First Nations people used this steep escarpment as a buffalo jump. Along the first section of the pathway, look for two signs of work undertaken to stabilize the slope. On the uphill side of the path large rocks have been wrapped in wire to keep the slope from sliding onto the path. Higher up the escarpment a cement-like substance has been applied to the steep slope to try and prevent further sliding.

If accessibility on this first section of the Sunnyside Pathway is a challenge you can detour on the following route. Continue along 3rd Avenue from the gargoyles to 5A Street. Turn left and walk north to 9th Avenue. Turn right and follow 9th Avenue east to 4A Street where the Sunnyside Pathway comes down the slope to the base of the escarpment.

After a few steps along the Sunnyside Pathway you will be overlooking the back yards of the houses on the north side of 3rd Avenue. When the trees and bushes on the slope are in leaf these houses are barely visible from the path. After a short distance look for more houses facing towards the base of the escarpment. These north-facing houses are on the south side of 9th Avenue. At one time there were numerous houses on the north side of this avenue both west and east of 5A Street but they had to be removed because of the unstable slope. On Sunnyside Walk 2 – Sunnyside Short Loop you will be walking along that section of 9th Avenue.

The path levels off after the short ascent and you pass a trail leading up the escarpment. This is part of a new system of trails designed to reduce the number of trails and the extensive erosion of the slope. As the path starts to descend you can see some of the houses at the top of the escarpment on Crescent Road. Crescent Road is on the route for SAIT/ACA/Jubilee Station Walk 3 – Rosedale & Crescent Heights. A branch of the path leads to the right to 9th Avenue just east of 5th Street. Your route stays on the main path.

At the corner of 9th Avenue and 4A Street the path passes another trail leading up the escarpment. You then pass a small park and Hillhurst Sunnyside Community Garden on your right. A third trail leads up the slope near the garden. A narrow alley between you and the garden fence is used to reach two houses that no longer have front street access. They used to face onto 4th Street. A second alley on the south side of the two houses provides a second route for the residents of these two houses to reach Sunnyhill Lane one block north of 7th Avenue. Sunnyhill Housing Cooperative is between Sunnyhill Lane and 3rd Street.

Continue along the main path until you reach the north end of 3rd Street at the base of the escarpment. A paved path leads up the escarpment on the left passing underneath a long set of stairs connecting the base of the escarpment to Crescent Road. A streetcar line used to go up the escarpment in this location after travelling east along 2nd and 7th Avenues. At the top of the escarpment the streetcar line went east on 6th Avenue before going down the slope to Centre Street and heading back to downtown. Historic photo NA-2891-11 dated 1911 shows the first streetcar to travel on the route to Crescent Heights.

Turn right and follow 3rd Street south past the Calgary Curling Club building. At Memorial Drive turn right and start following the sidewalk west towards 10th Street (1.6 km). The housing on the north side of Memorial Drive is a mix of older homes, old and new apartments and some townhouses. On the south side of Memorial Drive is the Bow River Pathway. About 900 trees were planted on the north side of the Bow River between Hillhurst (Louise) Bridge and St. George's Island in the 1920s as a memorial to those who lost their lives in World War I. In 1960 the name Memorial Drive was given to this road replacing the four different names for the road, on the north side of the river. The names from west to east were Westmount

First streetcar to cover route to Crescent Heights, Calgary, June 22nd, 1911.
Glenbow Archives NA-2891-11

Automobile on Memorial Drive, Calgary, ca. 1913-1919.
Glenbow Archives NA-4099-5

Boulevard, Sunnyside Boulevard, Memorial Drive and Riverside Boulevard.
The removal of many of these trees started in the 1980s due to old age,
disease and road widening. New trees have been added as part of the
restoration of Memorial Drive. At the time of writing work continues on the

Landscape of Memory along Memorial Drive near Hillhurst (Louise) Bridge. *Poppy Plaza* adjacent to the old Fire Hall # 6 on the west side of the bridge will feature a plaza area with a wooden deck and a steel wall. The *Calgary Soldiers Memorial* was unveiled in April, 2011 on the west side of the fire hall. The route for Sunnyside Station Walk 5 – Bow River Pathway & West Hillhurst will go past *Poppy Plaza* and the *Calgary Soldiers Memorial*.

The historic photo of Memorial Drive on the previous page was taken from the edge of the Bow River looking west. From the photo you can see that a raised water level on the river could soon cause flooding problems.

One of the early residents of the house at 436 Memorial Drive was Cappy Smart, the renown chief of the Calgary Fire Department from 1898 to 1933. A carpenter named Thomas Smalley built the rather interesting looking house at 440 Memorial Drive in 1907.

As you continue further west along Memorial Drive look for two historic apartment buildings. Andrew Murdoch constructed the three-storey Donegal Mansions at 830 Memorial Drive in 1930. There is a historic information plaque beside the front door. One of the building's most prominent residents was former Alberta Premier John Brownlee. A second three-storey building called Glenwood Manor is on the northwest corner of Memorial Drive and 8th Street at 904-908 Memorial Drive. Andrew Murdoch also constructed this building in 1928. On the other side of Memorial Drive at 8th Street you can see the red Peace Bridge that opened in March 2012. Spanish architect Santiago Calatrava designed the bridge. The bridge crosses over the Bow River to a location just west of Prince's Island.

Your route continues west passing under the LRT bridge and a pedestrian bridge (2.8 km). After going under the bridges you pass the Brower House built in 1907 at 1052 Memorial Drive on the west side of 9A Street. Brothers Archibald Brower, a steam engineer, and Frank C. Brower, publisher of the Gazette, lived here for many years. Just past the house look to the right towards the side of one of the older brick buildings on the east side of 10th Street. The painted name of a former business (Uneeda Bakery - R.W. Long Prop.) has been restored on the side of the building.

At 10th Street you reach the traffic lights at the north end of Hillhurst (Louise) Bridge. The first bridge crossing the river at 10th Street was Bow Marsh Bridge, a wooden structure used from 1888 to 1906. The steel Louise Bridge was then in use from 1906 to 1927 before being replaced by the present-day cement bridge constructed in 1920-21. The bridge was named for the daughter of the provincial Public Works Minister, William Cushing. The cement bridge was named Hillhurst Bridge although the name Louise was still used. Today the name of the bridge is Hillhurst (Louise) Bridge.

Turn right and head north on 10th Street taking time to explore the interesting assortment of stores, eating establishments and coffee shops. There are several older commercial buildings on the east side of 10th Street.

The one-storey building with storefronts at 104 and 106 was built in 1919. The similar one-storey structures at 106A and 108 were also built in 1919. Black's Pharmacy and Post Office were the occupants of 106A from 1920 to 1982. The Irwin Block, a two-storey brick commercial building at 110 – 10th Street, was constructed in 1911. The building is named for John R. Irwin, the original owner. The Carscallen Block is the two-storey brick commercial building located at 116 – 10th Street. This building was constructed by Shibley Carscallen and his brother Phillip in 1911. The one-storey commercial building at 144 – 10th Street where Lido Café is located dates back to 1912. It was first named the Union Building.

If you had walked along 10th Street in the 1920s some of the businesses in these buildings would have included a shoemaker, tailor, delicatessen, barber, bank, druggist, post office, hardware, bakery, jeweler, meat market, plumber and laundry. At this time there were homes north from 2nd Avenue on 10th Street. A couple of interesting business names from the 1940s were Brown Derby Market and Green Lantern Library and Gift Shop. By the 1940s the business area had extended north to 3rd Avenue and included a Safeway Store at 148 – 10th Street. Sunnyside Walk 4 – Gladstone Road & Kensington Road and Sunnyside Walk 5 – Bow River Pathway & West Hillhurst give you an opportunity to explore the stores on the west side of 10th Street.

At 3rd Avenue you turn right and walk east one short block to 9A Street

East side of 10th Street at Kensington Road

(3.5 km). In this block you pass an older row housing building formerly called Wellington Terrace built in 1911. Wellington Walker and his wife Louisa were long-time owners of this building. The building is presently named Lunenberg Apartments. Cross 9A Street to Sunnyside Station. The southbound Somerset-Bridlewood train stops at the near platform. To catch the northbound Crowfoot train cross both sets of tracks to the far platform.

Route Summary:
1. This route starts on the east side of the tracks at 4th Avenue.
2. Walk northeasterly on 4th Avenue.
3. Turn right and walk south on 7th Street.
4. Turn left on 3rd Avenue and walk northeasterly to the start of the Sunnyside Pathway a few steps past 6th Street.
5. Turn left and walk along the pathway to 3rd Street.
6. Turn right and walk south on 3rd Street to Memorial Drive.
7. Turn right and walk west along the north side of Memorial Drive to 10th Street.
8. Turn right and walk north on 10th Street to 3rd Avenue.
9. Turn right and walk one block east back to the station at 9A Street.

Sunnyside Walk 2
Sunnyside – Short Loop

Walk Overview: This walk makes a loop along several tree-lined blocks in this older community. Points of interest include several pre-1920 commercial buildings, a school built in 1919 and an interesting assortment of old homes interspersed with newer townhouses or apartments. The shade provided by the large mature trees make this route a very pleasant walk on a hot sunny day.

Length: 2.6 km

Route Description & Accessibility: This flat route has good accessibility. The walking surface is sidewalks with a short section of brick pathway.

Food and Drink: After the walk you could head for Riley Park north of 5th Avenue and west of 10th Street to relax at one of the tables or benches. There is a grocery store adjacent to the station. On 10th Street and Kensington Road there are several choices of restaurants and coffee shops.

Washrooms: Riley Park has seasonal public washrooms.

Map References: Clear-View – 28, MapArt - 154
Rand McNally – 49 & 50, Sherlock – 27

20

Route Category: Walk – The route starts and ends at the station (no bus is required).

The Walk: Passengers getting off the southbound Somerset-Bridlewood train walk to the front end of the platform and cross the two sets of tracks to the starting point of the walk at the back end of the northbound platform. Passengers getting off the northbound Crowfoot train walk to the back end of the platform.

From the south end of the northbound platform at 3rd Avenue you walk one block in a southeasterly direction on 9th Street to 2nd Avenue. On the northeast corner of this intersection is the Vendome Block, a two-storey brick commercial building, constructed in 1912 by contractor George W. Rae. The origin of the name Vendome is unknown. A city heritage information plaque is attached to the outside wall of the building. North Star Grocery occupied this building from 1912 until the late 1980s. At the time of writing one of the businesses in the building is a coffee shop.

On the south side of 2nd Avenue across from the Vendome Block are two smaller houses. Someone with a sense of humour obviously placed the names on the buildings. The house to the right has the name Rose Cottage above the front door while the house to the left has the name Cottage

Sunnyside School was built in 1919. In 1956 three classrooms and a gymnasium were added to the original six-classroom building

Cheese above the door. Sunnyside Cottage School was located at 1006 –
2nd Avenue. A short distance west of the corner at 1035 - 1st Avenue is the
Upton Residence, a small single-storey house, constructed in 1908 by
tinsmith Frederick Upton. The house is one of the oldest residences in
Sunnyside.

From the corner by the Vendome Block, head northeasterly along 2nd
Avenue. After crossing 7th Street on 2nd Avenue the school field of Sunnyside
School is on your right. This bungalow school is at the east end of the one
block area adjacent to 6th Street. Three naturalized areas named Riverstone
Park, Prairie Patch and Aspen Woodland have been developed on school
grounds by the parents, students and staff.

At the northwest corner of 2nd Avenue and 6th Street is the building
formerly occupied by Sunnyside Grocery. This building is very representative
of the small community grocery stores scattered through Calgary's older
districts. At the time of writing the store was closed and boarded up.
Hopefully this example of an older corner grocery store will not be
demolished. Cross to the northeast corner of this intersection (0.4 km). Take
a moment to glance at the sidewalk stamp on this older sidewalk. It reads
Secound Avenue. About one hundred years ago one or more of the crew
working on the construction of this sidewalk must have had one of those bad
days when things at work just didn't seem to go right. Hopefully most of
these old sidewalk stamps in Calgary with their inscribed names, rightly or
wrongly spelled, can be preserved. Many of these little symbols of early
Calgary history have disappeared over the last few years with the
construction of new buildings or the upgrading of the sidewalks. Information
on some of the remaining older sidewalk name and date stamps found along
the walk routes will be included in the Calgary CTrain Walks books.

Continue in a northeasterly direction along 2nd Avenue for two more
blocks to 5A Street. Here you reach one of the naming anomalies for Calgary
streets. The road's name changes from 2nd Avenue west of 5A Street to 7th
Avenue east of 5A Street. Another older two-storey brick commercial block is
on the northeast corner of this intersection. Turn left at this corner and walk
north on 5A Street towards 9th Avenue. On the west side of 5A Street at 3rd
Avenue is New Edinburgh Park. The former slough once located on this site
was filled with debris from building construction and the land converted into
a park. In 1993 this park became Calgary's first pesticide-free park. At the
corner of 9th Avenue and 5A Street stop and look to your left (1.0 km). At one
time there were houses on the north side of 9th Avenue west of 5A Street. A
quaint collection of smaller houses is still located on the south side of 9th
Avenue facing towards the bottom edge of the escarpment. You can spend

Remains of the old sidewalk on the north side of 9th Avenue are a reminder of when a row of houses backed onto the bottom of the escarpment slope

a few minutes exploring west of 5A Street on the north side of 9th Avenue where there are remains of the old sidewalk that was located in front of the houses on the north side of the block. The area where the houses were located is now overgrown with trees and bushes. There were also houses on the north side of 9th Avenue east of 5A Street. The sliding of the escarpment slope necessitated the removal of all the houses on the north side of 9th Avenue.

Head east on 9th Avenue and turn right on 5th Street walking south one block back to 7th Avenue. On the northeast corner at 5th Street and 7th Avenue is an older building that is now a residence. This is the former location of Jenkins Groceteria No. 10. Henry Jenkins started Jenkins Groceteria stores in 1909. On the southeast corner there is a small park beside the bus loop for route # 405 Hillhurst.

Walk one block west along 7th Avenue, turn left on 5A Street and go one block south to 1st Avenue (1.5 km). On the southwest corner of 1st Avenue and 5A Street is a small building surrounded by fence with warning signs attached. This building is the Sunnyside Stormwater Pumping Station. The photo on the next page shows flooding in Sunnyside in 1916.

Bow River in flood in Sunnyside, June 26th, 1916.
Glenbow Archives PA-951-4

The Urban Bird Time Share on 1st Avenue

Turn right and walk in a southwesterly direction on 1st Avenue. After crossing 7th Street you are now walking along the other side of the Sunnyside School field. When you cross 8th Street make sure you are on the right or north side of 1st Avenue. Look for an old tree that has been extensively pruned. On the flat surfaces left after the pruning are several attractive birdhouses. These are the handiwork of artist Yvonne Martinez who used to live in the adjacent house. A sign on the tree identifies her artistic work as *The Urban Bird Time Share*. This is another example of the interesting little things you discover when exploring communities on foot.

Continue in the same direction on 1st Avenue crossing 9th Street and walk one more block to where the road ends. The CTrain tracks located beside 9A Street are on the other side of a metal fence. Turn right and follow a red brick path north beside the tracks and the fence. Cross 2nd Avenue at the pedestrian crossing and continue one more block on the brick path beside the CTrain fence. At the next corner you reach the station and the finish of the route at 3rd Avenue and 9th Street (2.6 km).

Passengers catching the northbound Crowfoot train use the platform on the near side of the tracks. Passengers catching the southbound Somerset-Bridlewood train use the platform on the far side of the tracks.

Route Summary:
1. From the south end of the station platform walk southeasterly one block along 9th Street to 2nd Avenue.
2. Turn left and walk northeasterly along 2nd Avenue to 5A Street.
3. Turn left and walk one block north on 5A Street to 9th Avenue.
4. Turn left and walk west one block on the north side of 9th Avenue.
5. Retrace your steps and go east one block on 9th Avenue to 5th Street.
6. Turn right and walk one block south to 7th Avenue.
7. Turn right and go one block west to 5A Street.
8. Turn left and walk south to 1st Avenue.
9. Turn right and follow 1st Avenue southwesterly to the tracks beside 9A Street.
10. Turn right and follow the walkway north on the east side of the tracks back to the station just past 3rd Avenue.

Sunnyside Walk 3
Riley Park & Westmount Boulevard

Walk Overview: The first portion of this loop route wanders through Riley Park and Senator Patrick Burns Memorial Gardens before heading south on 12th Street to Kensington Close. After heading west to 14th Street the route follows Westmount Boulevard and Memorial Drive east to 10th Street. The route concludes with a walk north along 10A Street on the way back to the station. Points of interest include Riley Park, Senator Patrick Burns Memorial Gardens and several historic buildings.

Length: 3.7 km

Route Description & Accessibility: Most of the route is relatively flat with a walking surface of sidewalks or paved paths. The ascents and descents on the trails in Senator Pat Burns Memorial Gardens are not very accessible. There is also a short set of stairs from 14th Street down to Westmount Boulevard. An alternate route to avoid the stairs is included in the text.

Food and Drink: Riley Park has tables and benches. There is a grocery store adjacent to the station. On 10th Street and Kensington Road there are several choices of restaurants and coffee shops.

Washrooms: Riley Park has seasonal public washrooms.

Map References: Clear-View – 28, MapArt – 154 & 164
Rand McNally – 49, Sherlock – 27 & 26

Route Category: Walk – The route starts and ends at the station (no bus is required).

The Walk: Passengers getting off the southbound Somerset-Bridlewood train, walk to the back end of the platform at 4th Avenue and 9A Street. Passengers getting off the northbound Crowfoot train walk to the front of the platform and cross the two sets of tracks to the starting point of the walk on the west side of the tracks at 9A Street and 4th Avenue.

Begin the walk by heading west one short block on 4th Avenue to 10th Street. Make a right turn and go north a few steps to the traffic lights at 5th Avenue. Cross 10th Street to the far northwest corner. Walk north a short distance to the southeast corner of Riley Park and follow a path leading into the park. This path joins a wider paved path after a few steps. In 1910 Ezra Riley donated 8.1 hectares of land for use as a park. The site of the park was once part of Cochrane Ranche. Development of the park included the planting of trees and shrubs in the first few years. In 1914 a toboggan slide was constructed on the escarpment to the north of the park. For some years the NWMP flagpole from Fort Calgary was located in the park.

View of Sunnyside district from North Hill, 1917.
Glenbow Archives NA-1416-1

The first cricket pitches in the park were developed in 1919. Cricket is still played in the park almost 100 years later. In the 1920s there was also an old war cannon in the park. The wider path along the edge of the park is an old road left over from an era when park visitors could drive into the park at the south gate and circle counterclockwise around the edge of the park and exit by the west gate.

From the southeast corner of the park turn right and follow the path north along the east side of the park. To the left in the summer are very attractive flower gardens where wedding parties often choose to take their photos. On your right you pass the Sundial of Hope placed here in 1993 by Child Find Alberta. When the path turns left at the northeast corner of the park you leave the path and angle to the right across the grass towards 10th Street.

Senator Pat Burns Memorial Gardens are on the slope on the west side of 10th Street adjacent to the park (0.4 km). This impressive rock garden was developed in the 1950s using sandstone acquired from the demolition of Senator Burns' home at 12th Avenue and 4th Street SW. Burns moved to Calgary from Ontario in 1890. He became a very successful entrepreneur with his business interests including P. Burns and Company Ltd, a company that became one of the biggest meat packing businesses in the country. A national historic plaque in the gardens recognizes Burns. At the south end of the gardens is a floral display depicting Senator Pat Burns' brand. There is also a plaque to recognize Alex Munro who served as Calgary's parks superintendent for 21 years. Alex Munro Park is on Edmonton Trail at 18th Avenue NE.

Visitors can follow a network of paths and trails through the gardens. The ascents and descents on the paths and trails in the gardens have restricted accessibility. If you are strolling through this park on a summer weekend watch that you don't wander through the midst of a group taking wedding photos. From the top of the gardens you will be close to the location where the photo on the previous page was taken. In the photo you can see where a road used to come down the slope on the east side of 10th Street.

After visiting the gardens return to the wider path in Riley Park and turn right walking west along the north side of the park. Near the parking lot you pass by the cricket clubhouse and the two cricket pitches. Look for the date on the clubhouse. The sport was also played in South Calgary and Elbow Park. A new pitch has been developed in Martindale. On the far side of the parking lot you rejoin the wider path as it goes up a short ascent. A locked gate between the west end of the parking lot and the wider path makes access through this area more challenging for those with wheelchairs or strollers. To your left after leaving the parking lot is an excellent and popular wading pool. The pool area has changing rooms and seasonal washrooms. There has been a wading pool in Riley Park for many years.

Cricket Clubhouse at Riley Park

Continue along the path as it turns left near the northwest corner of the park and heads south to exit the park at the west gate at 7th Avenue and 12th Street. Cross 12th Street to the northwest corner to where you are standing at the southeast corner of the Hillhurst School field (1.2 km). Hillhurst, one of eighteen sandstone schools built in Calgary, opened in 1911. The building's original design was the same as Colonel Walker School in Inglewood and Connaught School in the Beltline community. On the east wall of the gymnasium addition is a large mural painted by the children in recognition of the school's 100th anniversary.

Cross to the southwest corner of 7th Avenue and 12th Street. St. Barnabas Anglican Church is on this corner. The church is named for Barnabas, a Jewish Levite who was a member of a caste of priests. The name Barnabas means "son of encouragement" or "son of consolation". After the Resurrection, Barnabas became one of the more ardent followers of Jesus.

The sidewalk on the corner beside the church is dated 1912. The first Anglican church on this site was constructed in 1906. This small original church was replaced by a larger building in 1912. In 1957 a fire destroyed all but the church tower of the second building. The congregation rebuilt incorporating the tower as part of the present-day building. On the various plaques attached to the building are photos of all three buildings. The following photo shows the second church building with the tower that is now part of the third church building. There is a small graveyard on the east side of the church. Look for the church name inscribed on the sidewalk just south of 7th Avenue.

St. Barnabas Church, ca. 1930. Glenbow Archives PA-3689-155
The tower on the right survived the 1957 fire

29

Calgary Tigers playing football at Riley Park, 1913.
Glenbow Archives NA-1744-7

The route now heads south on 12th Street past the east side of Hillhurst Sunnyside Community Park. This park has a long history. In 1914 two skating rinks were developed in the park with one being used for hockey. The park also became very popular for team sports including football. At one time the park facilities included a grandstand for spectators.

Cross 5th Avenue and continue south on 12th Street. The former Hillhurst Cottage School building at 455 – 12th Street is now the home of the Alberta Wilderness Association. The building is one of only three cottage schools remaining in Calgary. The other two cottage schools are Grand Trunk on 5th Avenue west of 23rd Street NW and Capitol Hill on 21st Avenue NW between 14th and 15th Streets. At one time there were seventeen of these cottage schools. There were two architectural designs used in their construction.

Continue south on 12th Street passing the site where the former St. Paul's Methodist Church building was located at 421 – 12th Street. Cross Gladstone Road and continue south towards Kensington Road. Just north of Kensington Road you pass an ornamental gate built to restrict traffic through the community. On the gate is the name Oxford Street, the former name of 12th Street. There are similar gates at the south ends of 11A, 11th and 10A Streets. These streets were formerly named Norfolk, Beverly and Preston. On Sunnyside Walk 4 – Gladstone and Kensington Road, you will be able to see these names on the gateways just north of Kensington Road.

Walk a few steps west on Kensington Road and cross to the south side at the pedestrian crossing light (1.9 km). St. John's School is on your right.

The former Hillhurst Cottage School building is presently cccupied by Alberta Wilderness Association

This building is described in more detail on Sunnyside Station Walk 4 – Gladstone Road and Kensington Road. Head south on 12th Street to Kensington Close (the name has been changed from the original Bowness Road). On the south side of the street is the large brick Hillhurst United Church. The original congregation in this building was Hillhurst Presbyterian, first organized in 1907. Their initial building was constructed in 1908 and replaced by the present building in 1913 as the numbers of worshippers grew. By 1915 the church members were discussing amalgamation with the nearby St. Paul's Methodist Church. The two congregations joined some ten years later. Look for the cornerstone from St. Paul's set in the wall of the church hall.

From the front of the church, turn right and head west on Kensington Close to 14th Street. Turn left and walk south on 14th Street to a set of stairs leading down to the west end of Westmount Boulevard. This street name is probably derived from the Westmount district in Montreal. The noise of the traffic on this short stretch along 14th Street can be a bit annoying at busy times of the day. Nearby a tunnel leads under 14th Street. If you walk through the tunnel there is another of Calgary's street naming anomalies. Broadview Road is the street on the west side of the tunnel. Westmount Boulevard on the west side of 14th Street is one block south of the tunnel. Also of some trivial interest is that 14th Street from the south side of the

Mewata Bridge north to Berkley Gate in Beddington has no fewer than seven tunnels under the road. The bridge is named for its proximity to the former Mewata Park on the south side of the river east of 14th Street. Rev. John McDougall named the park in 1906. The name is a Cree word that translates as either "to be happy or joyful" or a "pleasant place".

If you require better accessibility than the set of stairs continue a short distance further south and turn left down a small descent to the Bow River Pathway. From there turn left and follow the path east to 10th Street. At that corner you cross to the north side of Memorial Drive to rejoin the main route.

From the tunnel your route heads east on Westmount Boulevard and when the road joins Memorial Drive you continue east towards 10th Street. Just west of 10th Street on the south side of Memorial Drive, you see the old Fire Hall No. 6 building. This building and the Bow River Pathway are on the route of Sunnyside Walk 5 – Bow River Pathway & West Hillhurst.

At 10th Street turn left and walk one block north to Kensington Road. Cross to the north side of Kensington Road and turn left walking one short block west to 10A Street (3.1 km). On the west side of 10A Street, just north of the Hillhurst Block on the corner, are two older buildings constructed in 1911 and 1912. They have been connected to make one building with the present occupant being a restaurant and pub.

Head north on 10A Street passing by the ornamental gate. Turn right at 3rd Avenue and walk the short block back to 10th Street. St. John's Catholic Church used to be located on the northwest corner of 3rd Avenue and 10th Street. The church building was destroyed by fire in December 2002. At the time of writing construction is now underway on a condo project for this location. Cross 10th Street at the pedestrian crossing light and continue east on 3rd Avenue to 9A Street (3.7 km).

Passengers catching the southbound Somerset-Bridlewood train get on at the near platform. Passengers catching the northbound Crowfoot train cross the tracks and catch the train at the far platform.

Route Summary:
1. From the north end of the platform go west on 4th Avenue to 10th Street.
2. Cross at the traffic lights to the northwest corner of the intersection.
3. Walk north along the west side of 10th Street and just past the alley turn left on the path entering the southeast corner of Riley Park.
4. Turn right and follow the wider path to the northeast corner of the park.
5. Leave the path here and angle to the right to the south side of Senator Burns Memorial Gardens.
6. Spend a few minutes exploring the trails in the Memorial Gardens.
7. Return to the wider path and follow it west along the north side of the park walking across a parking lot.
8. After the parking lot continue on the path to where it ends at the park's west gate at 12th Street and 7th Avenue.

9. Walk south on 12th Street crossing Kensington Road and continuing one block further to Kensington Close.
10. Turn right and follow Kensington Close west to 14th Street.
11. Turn left and walk south on 14th Street turning left down a set of stairs to reach Westmount Boulevard.
12. Follow Westmount Boulevard east and continue further east on the north side of Memorial Drive to 10th Street.
13. Turn left and walk one block north to Kensington Road.
14. Turn left on Kensington Road and then turn right onto 10A Street.
15. Walk north to 3rd Avenue and turn right following 3rd Avenue east crossing 10th Street and continuing east to the station at 9A Street.

Sunnyside Walk 4
Gladstone Road & Kensington Road

Walk Overview: The first portion of this loop route is along Gladstone Road. This rather quaint little street angles across the community in contrast to the square network of most other streets in Hillhurst. The second portion of the route passes by the shops, restaurants and coffee shops of Kensington Road and 10th Street. Several pre-1920 historic buildings can be viewed along the route.

Length: 2.1 km

Route Description & Accessibility: This flat route with good accessibility follows sidewalks through the district. Some sections of Gladstone Road are very narrow.

Food and Drink: After the walk you could head for Riley Park north of 5th Avenue and west of 10th Street to relax at one of the tables or benches. There is a grocery store adjacent to the station. On 10th Street and Kensington Road there are several choices of restaurants and coffee shops.

Washrooms: Riley Park has seasonal public washrooms.

Map References: Clear-View – 28, MapArt – 164
Rand McNally – 49, Sherlock – 27 & 26

Route Category: Walk – The route starts and ends at the station (no bus is required).

The Walk: Passengers getting off the southbound Somerset-Bridlewood train walk to the start of the route at the front end of the platform. Walkers getting off the northbound Crowfoot train walk to the back of the platform and cross the two sets of tracks to the starting point of the walk at 9A Street and 3rd Avenue.

Walk west on 3rd Avenue to 10th Street and cross to the west side of the street at the pedestrian crossing light. Make a right turn and walk north

The former Hillhurst Baptist Church was built in 1908

on 10th Street to Gladstone Road. This road may have been named for the former British Prime Minister William E. Gladstone. Turn left and follow Gladstone Road in a southwesterly direction as it crosses through Hillhurst from 10th Street to 14th Street. In the first block of Gladstone Road there is a bright blue building on your right. This is the former Hillhurst Baptist Church built in 1908 and enlarged in 1914. The original name of the church was Morleyville Road Baptist Church. Since the congregation disbanded in 1972 various organizations and businesses have occupied the former church building and the adjoining hall.

Continue walking along Gladstone Road. Gladstone is intersected at an angle by 10A, 11th, 11A and 12th Streets. There is a slight bend to 13th Street so the two roads meet at a right angle. You will pass two small parks beside Gladstone Road. Look at the sidewalk stamp on the south side of Gladstone Road where the road meets 1st Avenue at an angle. In 1926 a creative sidewalk contractor put the name Gladstone Road at an angle across the sidewalk to copy the angle of the two roads meeting. A few steps west of that corner, Gladstone Road bends to the right and meets 14th Street at a right angle (1.0 km).

Turn left and walk south a short distance on 14th Street to Kensington Road. On the northwest corner of Kensington Road and 14th Street is the former Alberta Government Telephones Sub-station/Louise Exchange constructed in 1922. Cross to the south side of Kensington Road and turn left walking east towards 10th Street. Kensington Road was renamed Centre Avenue in 1904 before reverting back to the original name by the 1940s. Kensington is named after the district of the same name in London, England. At one time there were houses and just a few businesses along this street. Today there are no houses left between 14th and 10th Streets.

St. John's School, a brick bungalow school built in 1916, is on your right just beyond 13th Street. The school is named for St. John, also known as St. John the Evangelist. He and his brother James, also known as St. James the Greater, were two of the disciples of Jesus. St. John's School is similar in design to the former Holy Angels School built in 1919 on Cliff Street SW in Cliff Bungalow. Look for the ornamental lions above the front door with chains protruding from their mouths to hold up the canopy above the entrance. The additions to St. John's were constructed in 1954 and 1967.

Continue walking east along Kensington Road. The Plaza Theatre on your right at 1133 Kensington Road dates to 1929. Prior to being converted to a theatre in 1934-35 the building was used as an automobile garage. The Plaza is the last operational neighbourhood movie house in Calgary. In the 1940s the neighbourhood movie houses included the Crescent at 1718

Plaza Theatre

Centre St North, the Garry at 1229 - 9th Avenue East,the Isis at 1106 - 1st Street SW, the Kinema at 1805 - 14th Street SW and the Tivoli at 4th Street and 21st Avenue SW. Pages Bookstore just west of the Plaza Theatre is located in a former Calgary Public Library building.

The Hayden Block on your left at 1134-1136 Kensington Road is a two-storey commercial block built in 1912. Edward Hayden was a contractor who moved from Nova Scotia to Calgary. In the past few years the tenants have been primarily restaurants or pubs. The King George Lodge No. 59 building also on your left at 1126 Kensington Road was constructed in 1926. The masons used the building for their Lodge for close to sixty years. One of the present occupants is a coffee shop. The Arnell Block on the left at 1122 Kensington Road was built in 1911. Over the years this building has had various tenants and even a temporary name change.

There are two small older buildings behind the Hillhurst Block that were mentioned on Walk 3. At the corner of 10th Street and Kensington Road (1.6 km) turn left and walk north along the west side of 10th Street. Take the time to explore the various businesses along 10th Street. The east side of 10th Street is explored on Sunnyside Walk 1 – Sunnyside Long Loop. Cross to the east side of 10th Street at the pedestrian crossing light at 3rd Avenue and retrace your steps east back to the station (2.1 km).

Passengers catching the southbound Somerset-Bridlewood train get on at the near platform. Passengers catching the northbound Crowfoot train cross the tracks to the far platform.

Route Summary:
1. From the south end of the platform walk west on 3rd Avenue to 10th Street
2. Cross to the west side of 10th Street at the pedestrian crossing light.
2. Turn right and walk north to the east end of Gladstone Road.
3. Turn left and follow Gladstone Road southwesterly to 14th Street.
4. Turn left and walk south to Kensington Road.
5. Turn left and follow Kensington Road east to 10th Street.
6. Turn left and follow the west side of 10th Street north to 3rd Avenue.
7. Cross to the east side of 10th Street at the pedestrian crossing light and retrace your steps east along 3rd Avenue back to the station.

Sunnyside Walk 5
Bow River Pathway & West Hillhurst

Walk Overview: In the first half of the walk this loop route follows the Bow River Pathway from 10th Street to a pedestrian overpass at 21st Street. After crossing to the north side of the overpass the route wanders through a small section of West Hillhurst and then through Hillhurst on the way back to the station. Points of interest include views of the Bow River and a mix of older homes and commercial buildings.

Length: 6.1 km

Route Description & Accessibility: Most of this relatively flat route is on paved paths or sidewalks with good accessibility. There are short descents/ascents where the Bow River Pathway goes under Hillhurst (Louise) Bridge at 10th Street and Mewata Bridge on 14th Street. Both sides of the pedestrian overpass crossing Memorial Drive at 21st Street have long approach ramps.

Food & Drink: After the walk you could head for Riley Park north of 5th Avenue and west of 10th Street to relax at one of the tables or benches. There is a grocery store adjacent to the station. Along the route you pass a coffee shop and a café. On 10th Street and Kensington Road there are several choices of restaurants and coffee shops.

Washrooms: Riley Park has seasonal public washrooms.

Map References: Clear-View – 28 & 27, MapArt – 164
Rand McNally – 49, Sherlock – 27 & 26

Route Category: Walk – The route starts and ends at the station (No bus is required).

The Walk: Passengers getting off the southbound Somerset-Bridlewood train walk to the start of the route at the front end of the platform. Walkers

Calgary municipal railway car # 1 on Louise Bridge, 1910.
Glenbow Archives NA-5543-4

getting off the northbound Crowfoot train walk to the back end of the platform and cross the two sets of tracks to the starting point of the walk at 9A Street and 3rd Avenue.

Walk west on 3rd Avenue to 10th Street. Turn left and walk south on the east side of 10th Street to Memorial Drive. A description of the older buildings on the east side of 10th Street is included with Sunnyside Station Walk 1 - Sunnyside Long Loop. You walk past the buildings on the west side of 10th Street on Sunnyside Walk 4 - Gladstone Road & Kensington Road. At 10th Street and Memorial Drive use the traffic lights to cross to the southeast corner of the intersection (0.5 km).

At the time of writing the pathway underpass for Hillhurst (Louise) Bridge is closed during the construction of *Poppy Plaza* beside the bridge. The plaza is being developed as one of the projects for the *Landscape of Memory*. Until the construction is finished cross to the west side of 10th Street at the traffic lights and walk west past the former Fire Hall # 6 on the south side of Memorial Drive. When the underpass reopens walk west under the bridge stopping to look at *Poppy Plaza*. On the west side of the bridge there will be a wood deck area and sloping steel walls and large steel letters spelling Memorial.

Fire Hall No. 6 located just to the west of the southwest corner of the intersection, housed the Calgary Fire Department from 1910 to 1964. After a fire in 1974 the old fire hall was renovated and used for storage of city vehicles. The Calgary Area Outdoor Council is a current tenant in the building. City Parks and Recreation operated an Outdoor Resource Centre in the building for a few years.

Walk west from the fire hall to The Calgary Soldiers Memorial, a commemorative area unveiled in April, 2011. Continue west on the path to a short descent/ascent as the path goes under Mewata Bridge (1.3 km). This bridge was constructed in 1954. Across the river to the left you can see the elevated Sunalta Station, the first station after leaving downtown on the west line of the LRT. On your right you will pass the CBC building where a very popular Stampede breakfast is held. Broadview Soccer Field is on your right west of 19th Street. When the path reaches a pedestrian overpass look for ospreys on top of a wooden nesting pole just west of the overpass. Cross the pedestrian overpass to Brownsea Drive at 21st Street (2.3 km) in the community of West Hillhurst.

The land for this community was annexed in 1907 although most of the development did not take place until after 1945. Turn right and follow Brownsea Drive east past the Calgary headquarters buildings of the Girl Guides of Canada and the Boy Scouts of Canada Calgary. The name Brownsea Drive was chosen for this short one block road through the efforts of the Boy Scouts. In 1907, Lord Baden-Powell, the founder of the Boy Scouts organization, lead a group of twenty boys on a camping trip to Brownsea Island, England

Turn left at the west end of Broadview Field and walk north one short block to Broadview Road. Soccer has been played at Broadview Park since the 1950s. Turn right and walk east on Broadview Road one block to 19th Street. Turn left and head north on 19th Street. After crossing Bowness Road and Westmount Road you reach the traffic lights at Kensington Road. The name Bowness Road goes from 14th Street west to Crowchild Trail. There is a short section of road with the same name west of Crowchild Trail. The name then disappears until it appears again at 37th Street. From there Bowness Road twists and turns to where it ends in the Bowness district near 85th Street and 44th Avenue NW.

Continue north on 19th Street from Kensington Road. West Hillhurst is one of the communities in Calgary where wartime homes were built. You will see some of these homes as you walk along 19th Street. Other communities in Calgary with wartime homes are Capitol Hill, Renfrew and Balmoral near Edmonton Trail. Over 30,000 of these one storey or one and a half storey homes were built across Canada between 1941 and 1947 by Wartime Housing Limited that later became CMHC. The homes provided affordable housing for returning war veterans and their families.

There is a two block commercial area on the west side of 19th Street between 1st and 3rd Avenues. The businesses include a coffee shop and a café. Continue north to a set of traffic lights with 5th Avenue on your left and 6th Avenue on your right (3.7 km). Turn right and walk east on 6th Avenue. On your left are the West Hillhurst Community Hall and Arena and the Bowview Outdoor Swimming Pool. Across the park on 8th Avenue, one of the former Riley family homes was located near the present location of Bethany Care Centre. You re-enter Hillhurst as you cross over 18th Street.

Continue east a few more steps on 6th Avenue past the north side of Queen Elizabeth High School. The first school on this site was Bowview School constructed in 1910 as a boarding school. A three-storey school building then opened in 1930. When a large addition was added in 1953, the school was renamed to commemorate the coronation of Queen Elizabeth that same year. Turn right after passing the north side of the school and start walking south along the east side of the school. Near the south end of the high school building look for the old Bowview name above the doorway of the building. The date 1930 is also visible near the doorway. South of the high school is Queen Elizabeth Elementary School.

Another point of interest is the line of trees extending north-south along the east side of the schools. These trees were along one side of a road leading to Pauleson's Dairy Farm. A corresponding row on the west side of the road had to be removed when the schools were built.

At the playground for the elementary school turn right and exit the school grounds onto 18th Street. Turn left and walk south to 2nd Avenue where you

This original Bow View School sign and a 1930 date sign are on the east side
of the present-day Queen Elizabeth School near one of the entrances

turn left and start walking east towards 15th Street. Look for one very
interestingly shaped house on the south side of 2nd Avenue facing towards
the school field. At the intersection of 15th Street and 2nd Avenue the
sidewalks on the southwest and southeast corners are both dated 1913
(4.9 km) giving you an indication of when many of the homes along 15th
Street were built. On the northwest corner contractors kept the original date
stamp for the sidewalk in place while constructing a newer sidewalk around
it. From the corner, walk north on 15th Street towards 6th Avenue. A group of
houses on the west side of the street have a cement wall in front with the
lots raised above the street level. On the east side of the street one house
has steps leading down to the lot located below street level.

At 626 – 15th Street you pass a stained glass business located in an older
commercial building that once operated as Plaza Grocery. Turn right on 6th
Avenue walking east towards 14th Street. Cross to the east side of 14th
Street (5.3 km). On the east side of 14th Street the avenue's name changes
back to 5th Avenue. On the northeast corner is Hillhurst Sunnyside
Community Park and hall. This older community park is described in
Sunnyside Walk 3 – Riley Park and Westmount Boulevard.

Two older commercial buildings on 5th Avenue

Continue walking east on 5th Avenue towards 10th Street. East of 12th Street you pass two older commercial buildings. The Hunter Block (formerly Riley Park Grocery and Confectionary) is now a flower store. John R. Hunter, a building contractor, built this block in 1908. The former Park Gift Shop at 1207 is now an art supply store. One very interesting sidewalk stamp is on the southeast corner of 11A Street and 5th Avenue. The original mistake made in the stamp is still visible after an attempt was made to correct the mistake. At the traffic lights at 10th Street, cross to the east side of the street. Turn right and walk a few steps south to 4th Avenue. Turn left and walk one block to the north end of the station (6.1 km).

Passengers catching a southbound Somerset-Bridlewood train use the near platform. Passengers catching a northbound Crowfoot train cross the two sets of tracks to the far platform.

Route Summary:
1. From the south end of the platform walk west on 3rd Avenue to 10th Street.
2. Turn left and walk south on 10th Street to Memorial Drive.
3. Cross to the southeast corner of the intersection.
4. Angle to the left and then turn right to follow the Bow River Pathway under Hillhurst (Louise) Bridge.
5. Walk west on the Bow River Pathway going under Mewata Bridge.

6. Continue west to a pedestrian overpass. Cross the overpass to the north side of Memorial Drive near 21st Street.
7. Turn right and walk one block east on Brownsea Drive to 20th Street.
8. Turn left and walk one block north to Broadview Road.
9. Turn right and walk one block east to 19th Street.
10. Turn left and walk north on 19th Street to the intersection where 5th Avenue is on your left and 6th Avenue is on your right.
11. Turn right and follow 6th Avenue east past 18th Street to the northeast corner of Queen Elizabeth High School.
12. Turn right and walk south along the east side of the high school and the elementary school.
13. Turn right at the south side of the elementary school to reach 18th Street.
14. Turn left and follow 18th Street south to 2nd Avenue.
15. Turn left and walk east on 2nd Avenue to 15th Street.
16. Turn left and head north on 15th Street to 6th Avenue.
17. Go right on 6th Avenue and continue east past 14th Street as the name changes to 5th Avenue.
18. When you reach 10th Street cross to the east side at the traffic lights.
19. Turn right and then turn left on 4th Avenue to return to the station.

Sunnyside Walk 6
Nose Hill Park (Rubbing Stone Hill)

Walk Overview: This route begins and ends with an out-and-back section on a paved path followed by a loop through the park on trails. Due to the proliferation of trails leading away from the parking lot across the slopes of the park, you may want to ignore the suggested route and choose your own trails to explore. Points of interest include a glacial erratic and the view from the top of the hill. The eastern slope of the park is grassland with scattered trees or shrubs. A shallow ravine extends down the slope on the south side of an old road that climbs to the top of the hill.

Length: 3.3 km

Route Description & Accessibility: After following a paved path to the park from the bus stop, accessibility becomes very poor as you follow uneven surfaces on an old gravel road and on trails. For most of the walk you are either climbing the steep slope towards the top of the hill or descending back down the slope towards the parking lot. There is no good alternate route to reach the top of the hill.

Food and Drink: After the walk you could head for Riley Park north of 5th Avenue and west of 10th Street to relax at one of the tables or benches. There are no food stores, restaurants or coffee shops along this route. Another option is to visit one of the coffee shops or restaurants close to the station.

Washrooms: There are no public washrooms on this route.

Map References: Clear-View – 11, MapArt – 144
Rand McNally – 27, Sherlock – 19, 18 & 10

Route Category: Bus/Walk/Bus – Ride the bus to the start of the route and when finished the walk, ride the bus back to the station.

Bus Directions from the station to the start of the walk: Passengers getting off the southbound Somerset-Bridlewood train walk to the front end of the platform at 9A Street and 3rd Avenue. Passengers getting off the northbound Crowfoot train walk to the back end of the platform and cross the two sets of tracks to the west side. Walk west one short block on 3rd Avenue to 10th Street. Turn right and catch bus # 4 Huntington at bus stop 8045 on the west side of the Safeway store and parking lot. Get off the bus at stop 8997 on eastbound Norfolk Drive at Norfolk Way. Look for the Egerts Park sign. This stop is 18 minutes (weekends) or 19 minutes (weekdays) from the station. The bus frequency is 20 minutes during mid-day on weekdays and 25 minutes on Saturdays and Sundays.

The Walk: The community of North Haven was developed in the 1950s and 60s. The land for the south portion of this community was annexed in 1910 while the north portion was not annexed until 1953. Cross to the north side of Norfolk Drive and follow a paved path leading northwesterly through a green space. The path soon splits. The right branch leads up to a path along the east side of 14th Street. Take the left branch and walk through a tunnel underneath 14th Street (0.2 km). The paved path ends at the west end of the tunnel.

This is one of four tunnels that connect the communities east of 14th Street with Nose Hill Park. One of these tunnels is a short distance south of this tunnel near North Haven Drive. The trail from that tunnel enters Nose Hill Park just to the north of an old gravel pit road leading west up the hill from 14th Street. The third tunnel is connected to a path leading west from Hunterview Drive just north of 72nd Avenue. The fourth tunnel goes under 14th Street just south of Berkley Gate.

Nose Hill Park covers over 1100 hectares. Teepee rings, cairns and various stone artifacts have been found in over forty prehistoric sites in the area of present-day Nose Hill Park or on land surrounding the park. Some of these sites date back close to 8,000 years. There is evidence from his journals that David Thompson travelled through this area in 1800. After many years of being occupied by gravel companies and various landowners, the city and citizens began working in 1972 to preserve this area as a park.

The Friends of Nose Hill Park Society was instrumental in achieving this goal. The park was officially dedicated in 1992.

Rubbing Stone area of Nose Hill Park

Several dirt trails branch off from the tunnel exit. Take the trail to the right. It leads up a short ascent and passes a large rock with a plaque commemorating the opening of the park. Just beyond the plaque is the parking lot for this area of the park.

Cross to the far corner of the parking lot and go up another small ascent to where several trails lead towards an old road that winds its way to the former gravel pit at the top of the hill. Follow this road towards the top of the hill. As you near the top there is a glacial erratic on your right (0.8 km). This is one of the erratics that was carried to the Calgary area from close to Jasper during a period of massive glaciation. Within the Calgary city limits there is a second erratic in Confluence Park beside Beddington Trail and a third erratic adjacent to the Bridlewood Wetlands. The most well known erratic in Southern Alberta is Big Rock to the west of Okotoks.

When the road nears the top of the hill you reach a junction where the road splits. Turn left at the junction and continue on the road to the top of the hill. From the reasonably flat hilltop you can see buildings in the distance in the community of Edgemont. At the top of the hill you are on the north side of a former gravel pit. Turn left and follow a trail eastbound along the north side of the gravel pit. As the trail reaches the top edge of the east-facing slope you turn right. The trail passes to the right of a raised area that was on the outer edge of the gravel pit. Leave the trail here and climb up onto this raised area. From here you have an excellent view of downtown Calgary and towards the east. Another old road leading up to the gravel pit can be seen to the south of your location. Park visitors can park along this road or use a parking lot that overlooks 14th Street. From your location the trail you were on turns west heading towards that gravel pit road.

From the viewpoint select one of the many trails leading down the slope towards the parking lot (2.1 km). From the parking lot retrace your earlier route back through the tunnel (3.0 km) and along the short section of pathway back to Norfolk Drive and the end of the walk.

Bus Directions from the end of the walk to the station: To return to Sunnyside Station turn right on Norfolk Drive and walk a short distance west to bus stop 8996 just past Nottingham Road (3.3 km). Catch westbound bus # 5 North Haven for the return trip. On 10th Street, get off at bus stop 5246 at 5th Avenue. Walk south a short distance to 3rd Avenue and cross to the east side of 10th Street at the pedestrian crossing light. Walk the short block east on 3rd Avenue to 9A Street. The stop on 10th Street is a scheduled 20 minutes (on weekdays) and 18 minutes (on weekends) from the stop on Norfolk Drive. The frequency of the bus is 20 minutes during mid-day on weekdays and 25 minutes on Saturdays and Sundays.

Passengers catching the southbound Somerset-Bridlewood train use the near platform. Passengers catching the northbound Crowfoot train cross the tracks to the far platform.

Route Summary:

1. Walk west from the station on 3rd Avenue to 10th Street.
2. Catch a northbound bus # 4 Huntington at stop 8045 on 10th Street .
2. Get off the bus at stop 8997 on eastbound Norfolk Drive just east of Norfolk Way in the North Haven community.
3. Cross to the north side of Norfolk Drive and follow a path northwesterly through a green space.
4. When the path splits take the left branch through a tunnel under 14th Street into Nose Hill Park.
5. Take a trail to your right on the west side of the tunnel. Follow the trail up a small ascent to a parking lot.
6. Cross diagonally across the parking lot and climb another short ascent towards some information boards.
7. From the boards choose a trail that leads over to an old road that climbs the hill.
8. Near the top of the hill you reach a junction. Turn left and continue on the road to the top of the hill.
9. Turn left and follow a trail along the north side of an old gravel pit. The trail turns right when it reaches the top edge of the east-facing slope.
10. The trail leads to where you can leave the trail and climb up a few

steps to a viewpoint on your left.

11. From here pick one of the many trails leading downhill towards the parking lot.
12. From the parking lot retrace your steps back to Norfolk Drive.
13. Turn right on Norfolk Drive and walk to bus stop 8996 at Nottingham Road.
14. Catch westbound bus # 5 North Haven and get off at bus stop 5246 on 10th Street at 5th Avenue.
15. Walk south to 3rd Avenue, cross 10th Street and follow 3rd Avenue back to the station.

3rd Avenue by Sunnyside Station

Chapter Two
SAIT/ACAD/Jubilee Station

Station Information: This centre platform station is beside SAIT Way just south of 14th Avenue on the east side of 14th Street. SAIT Polytechnic is north of the station. SAIT was rebranded as SAIT Polytechnic in 2004. In this chapter the shortened name of SAIT will be used. ACAD (Alberta College of Art and Design) and the Southern Alberta Jubilee Auditorium are located south of the station.

The exit from the west end of the platform is at ground level. Use caution when crossing the tracks at this end of the platform. Exit from the east end of the platform is by enclosed overpasses leading left to SAIT and right to ACAD and the Jubilee Auditorium. Access to these overpasses is by stairs or an elevator. There is no escalator. There are enclosed waiting areas at both ends of the platform.

In 1916 Alberta established a Provincial Institute of Technology and Art. The first location for the Institute was Colonel Walker School in Inglewood. In 1919 the first step in the establishment of a permanent campus was the purchase of 110 acres of land on the North Hill from Ezra Riley. The main building now known as Heritage Hall opened in 1922. The Institute shared this building with the Normal School, a teacher training facility. From 1940 to 1946 the Royal Canadian Air Force operated No. 2 Wireless School in the building. The building was designated a Provincial Historic Resource in 1985 and renamed Heritage Hall. In 1989 the building was designated a National Historic Resource. Heritage Hall is located in the midst of a growing and dynamic campus.

Construction of the Southern Alberta Jubilee Auditorium started in 1955 as part of the province's 50th Anniversary. The building officially opened in 1957. Two long-time resident artistic companies are Alberta Ballet (since 1966) and Calgary Opera (since 1972). An identical Northern Alberta Jubilee Auditorium is in Edmonton.

The Alberta College of Art and Design building opened in 1973. ACAD is one of only four degree granting publicly funded Art and Design Colleges in Canada. An art college in Calgary was founded in 1926 and for many years was part of the Provincial Institute of Technology and Art. The college separated from SAIT in 1985 under the name Alberta College of Art. The name was then amended to Alberta College of Art and Design in 1995.

SAIT/ACAD/Jubilee Walk 1
Confederation Park

Walk Overview: The route is a mix of out-and-back sections combined with several loops. After leaving the station you pass through the west side of the SAIT campus and the east part of Capitol Hill community on the way to Confederation Park. The east boundary for Capitol Hill is 10th Street NW although some maps may show the area between 10th and 14th Streets as Pleasant Heights.

The total area of Confederation Park is 162 hectares. Confederation Park Golf Course is west of 14th Street. The portion of the park east from 14th Street and 24th Avenue to 7th Street and 30th Avenue has matured into a very picturesque location since development of the park began in 1967. In the warmer months you can often observe waterfowl in the pond area of the park. Tunnels in the park under 14th and 10th Streets allow park users to avoid the traffic on these two roads. This route wanders through the park from 13th Street to the east end of the park at 7th Street and 30th Avenue. From there the route makes a loop through Queen's Park Cemetery east of 7th Street and 30th Avenue before heading back to the station.

Length: 7.4 km

Route Description & Accessibility: The walking surface for most of the route is sidewalks or paved paths. There are a couple of locations where good accessibility is more challenging. The first is a short moderately steep descent/ascent on 13th Street as you enter or leave Confederation Park. The path through portions of the park has some short up-and-down sections. In the cemetery there is a short ascent and then a more gradual descent.

Food and Drink: There are picnic tables and benches in Confederation Park. The Stan Grad Building on the north side of Heritage Hall at SAIT has a food court area. Along the route you pass a deli before you reach Confederation Park. North of the SAIT Campus on 16th Avenue there are several coffee shops and restaurants.

Washrooms: The washroom building in Confederation Park near 7th Street and 30th Avenue is not always open. There are washrooms at SAIT.

Map References: Clear-View – 28 & 19, MapArt – 154
Rand McNally – 49, 39 & 40, Sherlock – 26, 18 & 19

Route Category: Walk – The route starts and ends at the station (no bus is required)

The Walk: After getting off the train walk to the west end of the platform and exit through the enclosed waiting area to where you are standing between the two sets of tracks beside SAIT Way.

Turn right using caution as you cross the westbound tracks and walk up a slight ascent to an intersection where SAIT Way meets General Motors Drive.

Cross to the north side of the road and turn left following General Motors Drive a short distance to where it joins 14th Avenue at an access road traffic light on the east side of 14th Street. On your right is the Clayton Carroll Automotive Centre Building named for former SAIT automotive service technician graduate Clayton Carroll. He donated $1 million to the institute's automotive training program. From the traffic lights turn right and follow the sidewalk beside the access road north to 16th Avenue (0.5 km). At the traffic lights at 16th Avenue, cross to the north side of the road. Continue straight ahead on the sidewalk beside the access road for 14th Street northbound. When the sidewalk reaches a bus shelter, turn right and climb a short set of stairs to the west end of the 1400 block of 17th Avenue. To avoid the stairs continue one block further north and turn right through a gateway in the traffic wall onto 18th Avenue. Walk one block east on 18th Avenue to 13th Street to rejoin the route. The 1400 block of 17th Avenue has some wartime houses. There are also some of these houses on 18th and 19th Avenues.

Walk one block east on 17th Avenue and turn left at 13th Street. Head north on 13th Street to 20th Avenue. The deli mentioned earlier is on the southwest corner. Cross 20th Avenue and continue north on 13th Street. After crossing 21st Avenue there is a descent to 22nd Avenue where a path on your right leads into Confederation Park (1.2 km).

A summer resident of Confederation Park

Confederation Park Tunnel under 10th Street NW

The Centennial Ravine Park Society was formed in 1966 to raise funds for the establishment of a park in recognition of Canada's Centennial in 1967. The group's efforts were very successful, resulting in the dedication of the park. The park is situated in a shallow ravine or gulley with slopes on both sides and water flowing through the park in a northeasterly direction. At the east end of the park the water flows underground into Calgary's storm sewer system. The golf course section of the park is between 14th and 19th Streets on the north side of Capitol Hill. Banff Trail Station Walk 1 – Banff Trail, Canmore Park and Collingwood makes a loop around the golf course. A tunnel leads under 14th Street at 24th Avenue beside the southeast corner of the golf course.

From 14th Street and 24th Avenue the park continues east to 7th Street by 30th Avenue. A pedestrian tunnel under 10th Street connects the two main areas of the park. Prior to the development of the park and the golf course the area was known as "the North Hill Coulee". West of 10th Street the park is bordered by the community of Capitol Hill (formerly Pleasant Heights) on the south and by the community of Rosemont on the north. The area for both communities was annexed in 1910. A few homes were built in Pleasant Heights by the 1920s but most of the development did not take place until the 1940s and 50s. Development in Rosemont started in the late 1950s. On the east side of 10th Street, the park is bordered by the community of Mount Pleasant on the south side and by the community of Cambrian Heights on the north side. The land for both these communities was also annexed in 1910. Mount Pleasant development started in 1912 while Cambrian Heights did not develop until the mid-to-late 1950s. Prior to the development of the park there were a few houses located within the area of today's park boundaries.

After walking a few steps from the 13th Street park entrance, the main path through the park is reached. Turn right and follow this path. The two seniors residences of Confederation Lodge and Parkview Village are on your right. As you walk along the main path look for the pedestal-like structure of stones on your left marking a location where a spring flows out of the ground. Just beyond this point is the wetlands area with a small island for the waterfowl and birds. The wetlands area was extensively renovated in 2005.

Continue east on the main path ignoring any paths leading left or right. As you approach the tunnel under 10th Street look for the Rosemont Community Hall on your left. The hall building that has been enlarged over the years was a former church building moved to this site from its previous location at 20th Avenue and 15th Street NW. Adjacent to the community hall is a ball diamond, a playground and an area for skating. A few picnic tables are next to the parking lot. There is also a toboggan hill near the community hall. A steel and aluminum sculpture entitled *Transition '67* by artist Enzo DiPalma is beside the hall parking lot.

The route makes a right turn and goes through the tunnel (2.0 km). Children enjoy shouting as they pass through the tunnel. On the east side of the tunnel take the right branch of the path. On your left you pass a small pond. After a few steps there is a four-way junction. Keep going straight ahead passing a toboggan hill on your right. At the next four-way junction again keep going straight ahead. There is a third four-way junction near a playground and some picnic tables. For the third time keep going straight ahead. The path then bends to the left around the edge of a parking lot and leads to a crosswalk just south of where 30th Avenue joins 7th Street (2.7 km). Cross the road and continue straight ahead on the path through an open green area between tennis courts and a ball diamond.

The path goes through a gateway in the chain link fence at the south end of Queen's Park Cemetery (3.0 km). This cemetery opened in the early 1940s. The path crosses a cemetery road and continues straight ahead. Your route turns left at the second cemetery road following the road as it climbs up a small ascent. Look for a path leading to the right into the Field of Honour area of the cemetery. After a few steps you reach a junction. Turn right and walk between trees lining both sides of the path to a commemorative area with a large Cross of Sacrifice honouring Canadians who lost their lives serving their country (3.5 km). This Cross of Sacrifice was dedicated in 1975.

Field of Honour at Queens Park Cemetery

Retrace your steps to the junction and take the left branch from the path you were on to the area in the Field of Honour that acknowledges the Year of the Veteran. On display you will find a Howitzer gun, an anchor and a propeller. The 5.5 inch Howitzer was used in battle in WW II. The naval and air force memorials were dedicated in 2005 (the Year of the Veteran). From this area keep walking straight ahead to a cemetery road. Turn left on this road and then make another left turn onto the road you left earlier to reach the Field of Honour. Make a right turn on the next cemetery road. This road leads to the cemetery road running parallel to the south fence. Turn left and follow this road downhill to the path and gateway where you entered the cemetery (4.2 km).

Turn right following the path back past the tennis courts and ball diamond. After crossing 30th Avenue angle to the right across the parking lot and follow the path leading from the parking lot towards the City Parks building that overlooks a ball diamond on your left (4.7 km). There is a seasonal public washroom in this building. Continue on the path to a junction. The path on the left from the junction crosses a bridge to your earlier route through the park. Beside this path is a flagpole with a plaque giving details about a time capsule.

Continue on the main path from the junction as the path starts to bend to the right around the bottom edge of a slope on your right. At a junction the right branch leads along the bottom edge of the slope to a parking lot. An ornamental flowerbed is on this slope in the summer. The left branch leads down a small slope to the tiny pond on the east side of the 10th Street tunnel. Leave the path at this junction and head across the grass towards a formal area where flagpoles with the flags of all Canada's provinces and territories are placed in a semi-circle around a map of Canada. The provinces and territories on the map are made out of stones native to each province or territory.

From this location head down the slope behind the flagpoles and join the path leading towards the tiny pond on the east side of the tunnel (5.1 km). Walk through the tunnel and retrace your route back to a four-way junction. Turn right at the junction and cross a small bridge. On the right is a small ornamental area dedicated in recognition of the efforts of former alderman Eric Musgreave (5.5 km). He played a major role in the development of the park.

Continue on the path taking the left branch at a junction. The path curves to the right below the edge of Roselawn Crescent. As the path nears the next junction look for a muddy and wet area on the left side of the path. A spring comes to the surface here and flows into the main water channel in the park. At the next four-way junction turn left and cross a bridge. The right branch from the junction leads to Roselawn Crescent. The centre branch from the junction continues to 14th Street. After crossing the bridge you reach a junction with the main east-west path through the park. The right branch leads to the tunnel under 14th Street. Take a few steps to the left on the main path to reach the point where you left 13th Street and entered the park (6.2 km). Walk back up 13th Street and continue south. At 18th Avenue turn right and walk one block west. Walk through the gateway in the traffic wall, turn left and walk south beside the access road on the east side of 14th Street of 16th Avenue. Cross to the south side of 16th Avenue and retrace your earlier route back to the station (7.4 km).

Route Summary:

1. Walk to the west end of the platform through the enclosed waiting area to the two sets of train crossing lights on SAIT Way.
2. Turn right using caution to cross the tracks and walk up a slight ascent on SAIT Way to General Motors Drive.
3. Cross to the north side of the road and turn left following General Motors Drive to where it joins 14th Avenue beside a northbound access road.
4. Turn right and follow the access road north to 16th Avenue.
5. Cross to the north side of 16th Avenue and continue northbound to a set of stairs beside a bus stop.
6. Climb the stairs to reach the cul-de-sac end of 17th Avenue.
7. Walk east on 17th Avenue.
8. Turn left and walk north on 13th Street.
9. Follow 13th Street down a descent north of 21st Avenue and turn right onto a path that connects to the main east-west path in Confederation Park.

10. Turn right and follow the main path until it goes through a tunnel under 10th Street. Ignore any paths leading left or right from the main path.
11. After going through the tunnel continue straight ahead. At the next three four-way junctions continue straight ahead.
12. Follow the path to where it bends to the left going past a parking lot to a crosswalk near where 30th Avenue meets 7th Street.
13. Cross the road and continue straight ahead on the path passing through a gateway into Queen's Park Cemetery.
14. Turn left at the second cemetery road and climb up a slight ascent and turn right onto a path leading into the Field of Honour area of the cemetery.
15. Turn right at a junction to observe the Cross of Sacrifice.
16. From the Cross of Sacrifice area retrace your steps to the path, turn right and then turn left on a path leading to the Year of the Veteran area.
17. Continue past this area and turn left on the next cemetery road.
18. At the next road junction turn left and then go right onto the next road.
19. This road leads to the south cemetery fence.
20. Turn left on the path going down a gradual descent to the cemetery gateway.
21. Turn right and follow the path back to 30th Avenue.
22. Cross the road and angle to the right across the parking lot to a path.
23. Follow this path and when you can see an area with provincial flags angle left across the grass towards the flags.
24. From the flags head down the slope to the path on the east side of the tunnel.
25. Go through the tunnel and retrace your route to a four-way junction.
26. Turn right and cross a small bridge.
27. Follow the path going left at a junction and continuing to the next junction where you turn left and cross a second bridge.
28. Go left at the junction after the bridge to reach the junction where you earlier followed the path from 13th Street.
29. Walk south on 13th Street and turn right at 18th Avenue.
30. Walk west to 14th Street and turn left heading south along the edge of the 14th Street northbound access road back to 16th Avenue.
31. Cross 16th Avenue and retrace your earlier route back to the station.

SAIT/ACAD/Jubilee Walk 2
Capitol Hill & Mount Pleasant

Walk Overview: The route makes a loop as it passes through the communities of Capitol Hill and Mount Pleasant. The area for these communities was annexed in 1910. At one time the area between 10th and 14th Streets was called Pleasant Heights. Today this area is part of Capitol

Hill community. A few homes were built in Mount Pleasant and Capitol Hill by the 1920s but most of the development did not take place until the 1940s and 50s. Near the halfway point of the route you leave Mount Pleasant as you cross 2nd Street NW. Some maps show Balmoral as a separate community east of 2nd Street but the Calgary Communities website indicates it is part of Tuxedo. Construction in this community started in 1912. The communities you walk through on this route are a mix of older houses, new infill homes, historic schools and churches. Much of the route is along tree-lined streets. Near the end of the route you wander south through the SAIT campus from 16th Avenue and 12th Street on your way back to the station.

Length: 6.6 km

Route Description & Accessibility: Most of this relatively flat route is on city sidewalks. There are a couple of short sections on grass. An alternate route to avoid the grass is included in the text.

Food and Drink: There is a food court in the Stan Grad Building on the north side of Heritage Hall at SAIT. Along the route you pass a deli and a corner grocery. North of the SAIT Campus on 16th Avenue there are several coffee shops and restaurants.

Washrooms: There are washrooms at SAIT. There are no public washrooms along the route.

Map References: Clear-View – 28, 18 & 19, MapArt – 154
Rand McNally – 49 & 50, Sherlock – 26 & 27

Route Category: Walk – The route starts and ends at the station (no bus is required).

The Walk: After getting off the train walk to the west end of the platform and exit through the enclosed waiting area to where you are standing between the two sets of tracks beside SAIT Way. Turn right using caution as you cross the westbound tracks and walk up a small ascent to an intersection where SAIT Way meets General Motors Drive. Cross to the north side of the road and turn left following General Motors Drive to where it joins 14th Avenue at an access road traffic light on the east side of 14th Street. The Clayton Carroll Building is on the north side of General Motors Drive. Turn right and follow the sidewalk beside the northbound access road to 16th Avenue. This section of the route is identical to the previous walk.

At the traffic lights on 16th Avenue, cross 16th Avenue and the overpass above 14th Street to the northwest corner of the intersection. Cross the road for vehicles turning right from the southbound 14th Street access road onto westbound 16th Avenue. Turn right and walk north on the sidewalk beside the access road. Turn left at a gateway in the traffic wall that leads you to the cul-de-sac end of 18th Avenue (0.9 km). In the 1500 block, one building of interest is an older house on your right. At one time Capitol Hill Confectionary operated out of the front porch area of this house. The resident, an employee of Canadian Pacific Railway, had constructed a scale model elevated railway track that made a loop around the garden area on the west side of the house.

At 15th Street turn right and walk north to the pedestrian crossing at 20th Avenue. On the southeast corner is the headquarters building for the Royal Canadian Legion Alberta-NWT Command. The church building that became Rosemont Community Hall was located on what is now the Legion parking lot. After crossing to the north side of 20th Avenue walk through the gateway in the chain link fence into the southwest corner of Capitol Hill Park. This one block sized park is one of Calgary's older community parks. Development of the park began in the 1930s with the planting of trees and shrubs along the four sides of the park.

Walk across the park to the gateway on the east side of the community hall. On 21st Avenue across from the hall is the former Capitol Hill Cottage School, one of only three remaining cottage school buildings in Calgary (1.3 km). There were seventeen two-room cottage schools built between 1910 and 1912 to provide space for the increasing number of students. This 1912 building with an open front verandah is different in design than the Hillhurst Cottage School on Sunnyside Walk 3 – Riley Park & Westmount Boulevard. The Capitol Hill cottage building has been used for about 60 years as a scout hall.

From the cottage school re-enter the park and angle left across the park to the southeast corner where there are traffic lights at 20th Avenue and 14th Street. If you need better accessibility than the grass in the park follow 15th

Capitol Hill Cottage School building

Water tank near King George School, May, 1939.
Glenbow Archives NA-3084-11

Street north from 20th Avenue, turn right on 21st Avenue and then right again at 14th Street to reach the southeast corner of the park at 20th Avenue.

Head east along 20th Avenue. On the southwest corner at 13th Street you pass a deli located in an older grocery store building that dates back to at least the mid-1920s. There are tables and chairs outside the deli. The deli is also on the route for the Confederation Park Walk. The building at 1221 – 20th Avenue was also a grocery store that has now become a private residence. On the southwest corner at 11th Street another older corner store is still operating as a store. On the southwest corner at 10th Street is the former Pleasant Heights United Church (2.2 km). The congregation then built a larger church to the south on the northwest corner of 19th Avenue and 10th Street. The older building now serves the community as a children's care centre. A Korean congregation now worships in the church on 19th Avenue. The former parishioners of Pleasant Heights United amalgamated with Rosedale United and became Wild Rose United. That building is on the route for Walk 3 - Rosedale and Crescent Heights.

Cross to the east side of 10th Street at the traffic lights and walk past King George School on the north side of the avenue. The construction of this sandstone school began in 1912 with the official opening in 1913. The building is similar in design to Ramsay and Sunalta schools. The school is named for King George V, the King of Great Britain and the Commonwealth from 1911 to 1936. At one time a large water tower stood in the field area to the north of the school. The 152 foot high tower was built in 1932 with a water capacity of 500,000 gallons. The tower was used until 1952. Demolition of the tower in 1966 took six hours to complete. On the north side of King George School is a sculpture by Calgary metal sculptor Geoff Sandhurst. The sculpture is based on a theme of *Under the Prairie Sky*.

Gargoyles on the St. Joseph's bell tower

Continue east on 20th Avenue passing another former grocery store at 917 – 20th Avenue that has been converted to a private residence. At 7th Street and 20th Avenue there is a rather interestingly shaped building (the Scandinavian Centre) on the southeast corner. Make a right turn and walk one block south on 7th Street and turn left onto 19th Avenue. Walk one block east to 6th Street (2.9 km). On the northeast corner is St. Joseph's Catholic Church constructed in 1914. The church is named for Joseph, the husband of the Virgin Mary and foster father of Jesus. Three points of interest to note are the cornerstone with the date in Roman numerals, the statue inset into the wall above the front door, and the tall steeple that has long been a landmark in this part of Calgary. Note the gargoyles on the church tower. The open space on the north side of the church was the former site of the original St. Joseph's School. The present day St. Joseph's School is at 5th Street and 24th Avenue NW. On the east side of the church a centennial garden was developed in recognition of the church's 100th anniversary.

Continue walking east on 19th Avenue to 2nd Street (3.5 km). Of interest at this corner are the four small parks at the intersection that form a circular green space named Balmoral Circus. William Reader, Superintendent of Calgary's Parks and Cemeteries from 1913 to 1942, played a key role in the development of this circle in 1934. There are only two such intersections in

58

the city. The second location, Beaumont Circle, is in the Regal Terrace community at 15th Avenue and 4th Street NE. The building on the northeast corner of Balmoral Circus, now a private residence, is a former scout hall.

Walk south on 2nd Street one block to 18th Avenue and turn left. Balmoral School is on your right between 2nd and 1st Streets. Balmoral was the last of the 19 sandstone schools built in Calgary between 1892 and 1914. The school is named for Balmoral Castle in Scotland, built in 1882 by Prince Albert for Queen Victoria. Balmoral translates as "farm of the big clearing". One notable feature is the school's clock tower that has never had a clock although an urban myth is that the clock was being shipped to Calgary on the Titanic. Former Alberta Premier William Aberhart was the first principal of the school. High school students were temporarily housed in Balmoral prior to the building of Crescent Heights School in 1929. The gymnasium addition at the west end of Balmoral was added in 1955. Balmoral Bungalow School constructed in 1913 occupies the northeast corner of the school grounds at 1st Street and 18th Avenue. The second of the two bungalow buildings that were on this site has been demolished.

Walk south one block on 1st Street. On the left is the Hicks Block, a two-storey commercial block, built in 1912 by Calgary dentist, Dr. William Hicks. Early tenants in the four storefronts included dry goods stores, confectioners and milliners. A branch of the public library operated in the building from 1913 to 1943 when Crescent Heights Library opened on the northeast corner of Centre Street and 12th Avenue. In the 1970s the Hicks Block was renamed the Kelly Block.

Continue south on 1st Street to the building on the northwest corner at 16th Avenue. The congregation of Crescent Heights Methodist Church built this church in 1908. When the Methodist, Presbyterian and Congregational churches joined in 1925 this building became the home of Crescent Heights United. In 1968 the congregation joined with the congregation of North Hill United (a few blocks south) and became Rosedale United. Today that building is named Wild Rose United Church. You will pass that building on Walk 3 – Rosedale and Crescent Heights. The former Methodist building on 16th Avenue is now the home of the Unitarian Church of Calgary. The original Fire Hall No. 7 opened in 1912 on the northeast corner of 16th Avenue and 1st Street. The fire hall was demolished in 1973.

Retrace your steps north on 1st Street to 17th Avenue. Turn left walking across the school grounds past the front doors of Balmoral School (4.2 km) to reach 2nd Street. There is a city historic plaque near the front door. Turn right and head north one block on 2nd Street to 18th Avenue. There are many older homes on the west side of 2nd Street between 16th and 19th Avenues. Head west on 18th Avenue towards 10th Street (5.6 km). This is a very pleasant section of the walk along tree-lined streets past a mix of older homes and some infill homes. On the northeast corner of 10th Street and

18th Avenue another former grocery store has been converted to a private residence. Continue west on 18th Avenue to 12th Street.

Turn left and walk south to 16th Avenue crossing to the south side of 16th Avenue at the traffic lights. Start walking south through the campus. The first building on your left is the Aldred Centre, named after John and Cheryl Aldred. John Aldred graduated from SAIT as a heavy-duty mechanic in 1968. The Aldred family donated $15 million in 2010 towards the *Promising Futures* campaign. This building with its impressive wavy roofline opened in 2012. On your right as you walk south is the Thomas Riley Building. The Riley family settled in Calgary in 1887. The family owned the land that became the communities of Hillhurst and Hounsfield Heights as well as the land that became the SAIT campus. The road going west parallel to 16th Avenue on the north side of the Thomas Riley Building is Fowler Drive. Dr. James Fowler was the institute's principal from 1941 to 1952. James Fowler High School on 4th Street and 40th Avenue NW near the northeast corner of Queens Park Cemetery is also named for Dr. Fowler. The road leading left on the south side of the Aldred Centre is Dr. Carpenter Circle named for Dr. W.G. Carpenter who served as principal of the institute from 1924 to 1941.

From the point where 12th Street ends you continue south on the walkway between the buildings. On your left is the Eugene Coste Building, named for the discoverer of natural gas in Alberta. Ross Road leads to the right from the walkway on the south side of the Thomas Riley Building. J.H. Ross was acting principal of the institute from 1919 to 1923. South of Ross Road on your right is another newer campus building, the Johnson-Cobbe Energy Centre. The *Promising Futures* Campaign received donations of $5 million each towards the construction of this building from Petroleum Engineering Technology graduates David Johnson and Murray Cobbe.

On your left as you pass the Johnson-Cobbe Energy Centre is the Stan Grad Building. The building was formerly called the Heart Building. This building adjoins the north side of the historic Heritage Hall. Petroleum Technology graduate Stan Grad made a $7 million donation to the *Promising Futures* Campaign. A visit inside this building is worthwhile. A popular relaxation area with chairs and tables is located at the south side of the Stan Grad Building beside the north wall of Heritage Hall. For many years this north wall was hidden behind an older nondescript campus building that was demolished to make way for the Stan Grad Building.

On the west side of Heritage Hall the section of road at the east end of General Motors Drive is called Boyce Crescent. J.F. Boyce was the institute's principal in 1917-1918. Outside the west doors of Heritage Hall is the 2009 granite sculpture entitled *Self Made Woman* by artist Paul Slipper who was assisted by Cameron Small and Amiel Logan. From Boyce Crescent you have two route choices to return to the station. The first option is to turn right walking along the north side of the Campus Centre going down a set of stairs and turning left on SAIT Way where you walk a few steps further to reach the station. The second option is to enter the Campus Centre. You follow the main hallway to the left until you reach the enclosed overpass connecting the Campus Centre to the Jubilee Auditorium and ACAD. From the overpass you descend a set of stairs to the station platform (6.6 km).

Route Summary:

1. Walk to the west end of the platform through the enclosed waiting area to where you are standing between the two sets of train crossing lights on SAIT Way.
2. Turn right using caution to cross the westbound tracks and walk up a short ascent on SAIT Way to General Motors Drive.
3. Cross to the north side of the road and turn left following General Motors Drive to where it joins 14th Avenue at the northbound access road.
4. Turn right and follow the access road north to 16th Avenue.
5. Cross to the north side of 16th Avenue and turn left to cross the overpass to the west side of 14th Street.
6. Follow the southbound access road north to a gateway in the traffic wall on your left. Go through the gateway to the cul-de-sac end of 18th Avenue.
7. Walk west on 18th Avenue and turn right at 15th Street.
8. Walk north to 20th Avenue, cross to the north side and go through the gateway in the chain link fence at the southwest corner of Capitol Hill Park.
9. Walk across the park passing by the east side of the community hall to a gateway by 21st Avenue.
10. After viewing the school on the north side of 21st Avenue, go back through the gateway and angle to the left to the southeast corner of the park to another gateway.
11. Cross 14th Street and head east on 20th Avenue to 7th Street.
12. Turn right on 7th Street and then turn left onto 19th Avenue.
13. Walk east on 19th Avenue to 2nd Street.
14. Turn right and walk one block south on 2nd Street.
15. Turn left and walk east on 18th Avenue to 1st Street.
16. Turn right and walk two blocks south to 16th Avenue.
17. Retrace your steps to 17th Avenue and turn left through the school field gateway and walk west past the front of the school to 2nd Street.
18. Turn right and walk one block north on 2nd Street to 18th Avenue.
19. Turn left and walk west on 18th Avenue to 12th Street.
20. Turn left and walk south to 16th Avenue crossing to the south side.
21. Walk south through the campus on 12th Street.
22. When 12th Street ends continue south between the buildings.
23. When you reach the Campus Centre either turn right and walk around the outside of the building to reach the station or walk through the building to reach the station

SAIT/ACAD/Jubilee Walk 3
Rosedale & Crescent Heights

Walk Overview: This route wanders through the communities of Rosedale and Crescent Heights. The first development in Rosedale started in 1929. Crescent Heights was first established as a village separate from Calgary before being annexed by the city in the early 1910s. Near the end of the route you detour past the front entrances of the Alberta College of Art and Design and the Southern Alberta Jubilee Auditorium. The largest part of the route is a loop with a short portion of out-and-back walking.

Length: 7.9 km

Route Description & Accessibility: Most of this route is relatively flat. On both sides of 10th Street there is a slight descent/ascent on the SAIT Campus and in the community of Rosedale. A long set of stairs in Rotary Park requires an accessibility detour. Details of this detour are included in the text. There is also a long downhill section on the SAIT campus near the end of the route. No easier detour route is included in the text. The walking surface throughout the route is a mix of sidewalks, paved paths, grass and trails.

Food & Drink: There are benches and tables in both Rotary Park and Crescent Park. The Stan Grad Building at SAIT has a food court area.

Washrooms: There are washrooms in the SAIT Campus buildings. Rotary Park has a seasonal washroom building beside the water park. Crescent Park has a washroom building although it was found to be closed in the middle of the day in August, so don't count on this building being open.

Map References: Clear-View – 28, MapArt – 154
Rand McNally – 49 & 50, Sherlock – 26 & 27

Route Category: Walk – The route starts and ends at the station (no bus is required)

The Walk: After getting off the train exit the station through the enclosed waiting area at the west end of the platform. Turn right on SAIT Way using caution as you cross the westbound tracks and an access road to a service area for the Campus Centre building. A few steps straight ahead takes you to a set of stairs on your right. The stairs can be avoided by continuing a few steps further to General Motors Drive. Climb the stairs and walk east on the sidewalk on the north side of the Campus Centre. A small parking lot is on your left.

In front of Heritage Hall, a soccer field named Martin Cohos Commons sits atop a large parkade structure built into the natural slope of the hill. Cohos is associated with the architectural firm of Cohos Evamy Partners. He has been very involved with SAIT both as an instructor and on the board of governors.

Front entrance to Heritage Hall

Continue walking east past the front of Heritage Hall. There is a National Historic Site plaque near the front doors (0.2 km). After pausing to observe the impressive front entrance you might want to enter the front doors to view the interior of the building. Note the interesting sculptures above the front entrance. On the north side of the older building, the Stan Grad Building, a newer structure, has been connected to Heritage Hall.

When you reach the southeast corner of Heritage Hall, make a turn to the left and then a turn to the right to start walking east between the Senator Burns Building on your right and the John Ware Building on your left. Information on Senator Pat Burns is included in Sunnyside Walk 3. John Ware was a former slave freed at the end of the American Civil War. After accompanying a cattle drive from Texas to Idaho, he ventured north to Canada on another cattle drive and chose to stay, establishing his own cattle ranch. It seems ironic that this excellent horseman was killed in 1905 when his horse stepped in a hole and fell. John Ware School in Palliser community in southwest Calgary is also named in his honour.

The Hospitality Management program operates a small bakery/meat market store just inside the southwest doors of the John Ware Building. The Food Management program also operates the Highwood restaurant in the same building. The restaurant is open from early September to late April during the time the students are attending SAIT. Culinary Campus downtown is another program run by Food Management. On the south side of the John Ware Building is a food garden operated by the students.

The sidewalk continues straight ahead past the buildings and then angles to the right crossing Dr. Carpenter Circle just before reaching 10th Street. Cross 10th Street at the pedestrian crossing light (0.6 km). Use caution at this crosswalk. Continue eastbound up a short ascent on 13th Avenue in Rosedale. Rosedale School is just past 9th Street. Turn right at 7A Street and walk south to the west end of Alexander Crescent (1.2 km). There are several possible origins for this street name. The first possibility is two early Calgary real estate developers, Harry Alexander and his cousin, George. The second possibility is Alexander Robertson, the son of William Robertson who came to Calgary in 1883. William Robertson owned the land that became the community of Rosedale.

Turn left and follow Alexander Crescent east to 4th Street (1.8 km). Of trivial interest is that almost half of the sidewalk stamps read Alexandra Crescent and not Alexander Crescent. At 4th Street turn right and then left at the next corner heading east on 11th Avenue as you leave Rosedale and enter Crescent Heights.

Crescent Park is on the east side of 3rd Street when you reach the end of 11th Avenue. A plaque near the southeast corner of the park indicates this was Calgary's first park on the North Hill. The land was dedicated for park use in the 1920s with the first tree being planted in the park in 1923. In the 1930s trees and shrubs were added along the edges of the park.

Continue east across the north side of the park to 2nd Street past the community hall on your right and the North Hill Curling Club on your left. This north section of the park also has a playground. The central portion of the park has playing fields while the south end by Crescent Road is more ornamental. Crescent Heights High School is east and south of the intersection of 11th Avenue and 2nd Street. More details about the school are included later in this chapter. If you require better accessibility than the grass in the park turn left on 3rd Street, turning right on 12th Avenue and rejoining the route at 2nd Street.

Turn left and walk north on 2nd Street crossing 12th Avenue. Look to your right at 13th Avenue to view an older grocery store on the south side of 13th Avenue between 2nd and 1st Street. At 15th Avenue turn right (2.5 km) and then turn right onto 1A Street. Turn left at 13th Avenue and walk east to the corner at 1st Street where you will be standing beside Wild Rose United Church. A large plaque near the front doors outlines the history of the United Church on the North Hill. Crescent Heights Methodist Church built a church on the northwest corner of 16th Avenue and 1st Street in 1908. When the Methodist, Presbyterian and Congregational churches joined in 1925 that building became the home of Crescent Heights United. In 1968 their congregation joined with the congregation of North Hill United who were

Wild Rose United Church

worshipping in the present Wild Rose United building. The church was renamed Rosedale United. When the members of Pleasant Heights United joined with Rosedale United congregation in 2002 the church was named Wild Rose United Church. Head south on 1st Street crossing 12th Avenue.

Continue south on 1st Street to Crescent Heights Baptist Church on the northeast corner of 1st Street and 11th Avenue. This congregation dates back to 1909. The original church building for this congregation was on the southwest corner where Crescent Heights High School is now located. The present brick building was built on the northeast corner in 1912. The original wooden church building was then moved to 1006 – 1st Street and became a private residence. You can see that the larger church building is a mix of older red brick from 1912 (evident on the north wall) with a yellow brick addition.

On the west side of 1st Street between 11th and 9th Avenues is Crescent Heights High School (3.2 km) opened in 1929. The forerunner of this school was Crescent Heights Collegiate Institute that began operating in 1913 as a part of Central Collegiate, the first public high school in Calgary. The school was renamed Crescent Heights High School in 1918. Until the present school was built students were housed in other buildings including Balmoral School on 16th Avenue NW. There have been numerous additions to the original building. Former Alberta premier William Aberhart was principal at

Crescent Heights from 1915 to 1935. John Laurie, secretary of the Indian Association of Alberta, taught at the school.

Continuing south on 1st Street you pass two old sidewalk stamps (1913) on the northeast and southeast corners at 9th Avenue and 1st Street. Another 1913 sidewalk stamp is at the next corner at 8th Avenue. Continue south on 1st Street to 7th Avenue. The sidewalk stamp on the southeast corner is of particular interest. It shows the date 1910 and the name Linclon Avenue instead of 7th Avenue. Presumably it was to have been spelled Lincoln Avenue.

Turn left and walk east one block on 7th Avenue crossing Centre Street at the pedestrian crossing light. Turn right and walk under a sandstone arch into the north end of Rotary Park. This 5.9 hectares park was developed in the 1930s and was first named Mount Pleasant Rotary Park. The park facilities include a newly renovated children's water park, a washroom building, a playground and picnic tables. Walk south through the park past the Rotary Park Lawn Bowling Club established in 1931. On the west side of the lawn bowling is an older brick building used by Calgary Emergency Services. South of the wading pool is the Mount Pleasant Tennis Club. The tennis club retained the original name of the park. It is not known what year the club was established although the first club championships were held in 1932. The clubhouse was constructed in 1953 with additions in 1962 and 1976.

On the escarpment at the south end of the park is a series of plaques outlining a brief history of early Calgary. This area has been named Jim Fish Ridge. You have an excellent view from this location of Centre Street Bridge. The bridge with its familiar lion and buffalo head sculptures opened in 1916 replacing a steel truss bridge. The first river crossing in this area was Fogg's Ferry. The panoramic view also includes downtown Calgary, the Bow River and the Rocky Mountains in the distance. Samis Road leads down the slope south of the park from 1st Street NE to Centre Street. Adoniram Judson Samis settled in the Olds area in 1893 and later moved to Morley. In 1904 he moved to Calgary and worked in real estate. He served as a city alderman from 1906 to 1912 and as city commissioner in 1913 and again from 1917 to 1922.

Turn right from the plaques and walk a few steps to a long set of stairs leading down to Centre Street. If better accessibility than the set of stairs is required retrace your steps back to the north end of the park, cross Centre Street and walk west on 7th Avenue back to 1st Street. Turn left and walk south to the top of the escarpment on Crescent Road. At this point you will rejoin the route.

Descend the stairs to Centre Street (4.1 km). Cross at the traffic lights to the west side of Centre Street and turn right. After a few steps follow a paved path leading to the left up the slope to Crescent Road. The streetcar from Sunnyside came down this slope from 6th Avenue and travelled across

Lincoln Avenue sidewalk inscription at 7th Avenue & 1st Street NW

Centre Street Bridge on the way to downtown. At the top of the slope you are on Crescent Road near 1st Street. Cross to the north side of Crescent Road and look on the nearby northeast corner of 1st Street and 6th Avenue for the name Somerville Avenue (1910) inscribed in the sidewalk.

Cross back to the south side of the road and walk west on the trail past the Church of Jesus Christ of Latter Day Saints building. At 2nd Street you reach the top of a long set of stairs leading up from Sunnyside community (4.7 km). Often you may see individuals or groups exercising on the stairs. From the bottom of the stairs a pedestrian overpass crosses Memorial Drive and connects to the pedestrian bridge over the Bow River to Prince's Island Park. On a rock near the top of the stairs is a plaque with information about McHugh Bluff. Felix McHugh came to Calgary from Ontario in 1883 and established his homestead at the base of the escarpment in the present day community of Sunnyside. McHugh Bluff extends west from Centre Street to 10th Street.

Cross to the north side of Crescent Road and enter the southeast corner of Crescent Park. After viewing the park go back to the south side of Crescent Road and continue west along the trail on the top of the escarpment. There are some interesting older homes on the north side of Crescent Road. In the past year or so, city parks have closed many of the trails leading down the slope and upgraded a few trails for use by walkers and runners. The trail makes a large sweeping curve to the left following the edge of Crescent Road. At 4th Street and Crescent Road you leave Crescent Heights and re-enter Rosedale. The new trail on the south side of Crescent Road is a vast improvement on the rather rough trail with protruding tree roots that preceded it.

Just before Crescent Road reaches 7A Street you turn to the right and for a short distance lose the excellent view as you pass the houses to your left along both sides of 7A Street (5.8 km). A few steps west of 7A Street you reach a road junction. The right branch curves to the right and heads north as 9th Street. Follow the left branch or Crescent Road as it makes another sweeping curve this time to the right and heads north.

At this point the view opens up again. At one time there was a road that came up the escarpment to Crescent Road from 10th Street. Look for Riley Park at the base of the escarpment on the west side of 10th Street. As Crescent Road turns north look down the slope to where the Northwest CTrain line crosses an overpass above 10th Street as the train navigates the slope between Sunnyside Station and SAIT/ACAD/Jubilee Station. Walk north on Crescent Road to 13th Avenue. Turn left down a small descent to the pedestrian crossing light at 10th Street and 13th Avenue (6.6 km). Again use caution at the crosswalk.

After crossing 10th Street walk a few steps west to Dr. Carpenter Circle. If good accessibility is required you retrace your earlier route back through the campus to the station. Turn left and follow the edge of Dr. Carpenter Circle as it curves to the right around the south side of the Senator Burns Building. At the junction with the access road to the parkade, turn left and follow the edge of Dr. Carpenter Circle downhill to a traffic circle where the road meets SAIT Way. Cross SAIT Way and continue southbound across a parking lot to where you are at the top of the escarpment overlooking Riley Park. Turn right and walk along the top of the escarpment to where Jubilee Crescent makes a turn around the south side of another parkade.

Continue straight ahead along the edge of Jubilee Crescent past the south side of the parkade and the Alberta College of Art and Design building. Continue straight ahead to the next point of interest. The large 8 metres high bronze equestrian statue at the top of the escarpment is Robert the Bruce, the 14th century Scottish king, on horseback (7.6 km). Calgary philanthropist Eric Harvie commissioned two castings of the statue. This Calgary statue was installed in 1967. The second statue was unveiled in 1964 at the Battle of Bannockburn site, near Stirling, Scotland.

From the statue continue west on Jubilee Crescent to the front doors of the Southern Alberta Jubilee Auditorium. Construction of this building started in 1955 with the official opening in 1957. The auditorium and an identical building in Edmonton were built in recognition of Alberta's Golden Jubilee in

1955. Turn right along the west side of the auditorium crossing SAIT Way and the eastbound tracks to reach the west entrance to the station (7.9 km)

Route Summary:

1. After getting off the train exit the station through the enclosed waiting area at the west end of the station.
2. Use caution as you turn right and cross the westbound tracks and an access road.
3. A few steps straight ahead leads you to a set of stairs on your right.
4. Climb the stairs and walk east along the sidewalk on the north side of the Campus Centre.
5. Continue walking east past the front of Heritage Hall on your left.
6. At the southeast corner of Heritage Hall, turn left and then turn right walking east between the Senator Burns Building on the right and the John Ware Building on the left.
7. This sidewalk continues straight ahead and then angles to the right crossing Dr. Carpenter Circle just before you reach 10th Street.
8. Cross 10th Street at the pedestrian crossing light and continue eastbound up a slight ascent on 13th Avenue.
9. Turn right at 7A Street and walk south turning left at the west end of Alexander Crescent.
10. Walk east on Alexander Crescent to 4th Street.
11. Turn right on 4th Street and then turn left onto 11th Avenue.
12. Walk one block east, cross 3rd Street and continue straight ahead on the grass across the north side of Crescent Park to 2nd Street.
13. Turn left and walk north on 2nd Street to 15th Avenue.
14. Turn right on 15th Avenue and then right again on 1A Street.
15. Turn left on 13th Avenue and then right on 1st Street.
16. Walk south on 1st Street to 7th Avenue.
17. Turn left and walk east on 7th Avenue crossing Centre Street at the pedestrian crossing light and turn right walking under an arch at the north end of Rotary Park.
18. Walk south through the park to the top of a long set of stairs leading down to Centre Street.
19. Walk down the stairs and cross to the west side of Centre Street at the traffic lights.
20. Turn right and after a few steps turn left following a path up a slope to Crescent Road.
21. Walk west along Crescent Road to a road junction just past 7A Street.
22. Turn left as you continue to follow Crescent Road as it makes a sweeping turn to the right.
23. Follow Crescent Road north to 13th Avenue.
24. Turn left and cross 10th Street back onto the SAIT Campus.
25. Walk a few steps west and turn left on Dr. Carpenter Circle.

26. Follow the edge of the road as it loops around to the right.
27. When you reach the access road to the parkade turn left and follow the edge of Dr. Carpenter Circle downhill to a traffic circle on SAIT Way.
28. Cross SAIT Way and continue southbound across a parking lot to the top of the escarpment overlooking Riley Park.
29. Turn right and walk along the top of the escarpment to where Jubilee Crescent makes a turn around the corner of another parkade.
30. Continue straight ahead on Jubilee Crescent past the Alberta College of Art and Design and the Southern Alberta Jubilee Auditorium.
31. Turn right along the west side of the auditorium crossing SAIT Way and the eastbound train tracks to reach the west entrance to the station.

View of Riley Park from Crescent Road

Chapter Three
Lions Park Station

Station Information: The station is located in Lions Park on the south side of 14th Avenue just east of 19th Street. The North Hill Centre shopping centre is across 14th Avenue from the station. The community of Hounsfield Heights is on the south side of the park.

The station has side platforms with a crossing for the tracks and 14th Avenue at the east end of the platforms. The west end of the platform has a crossing for the tracks. Use caution crossing the tracks. The platforms have unheated shelters for passengers. There are several buses that stop on 14th Avenue adjacent to the station.

Lions Park was developed in 1953 but reduced in size for construction of the Northwest C-Train line. Hounsfield Heights is named after Georgina Hounsfield, the wife of Thomas Riley. The land occupied by the community was part of the Riley family's homestead. Development of Hounsfield Heights began in 1906 after the city annexed the land. There are a few older houses in the community. The original North Hill Centre was constructed in the late 1950s and has undergone many changes since that time.

Lions Park Walk 1
Briar Hill, St. Andrews Heights
& Shagnessey Heights Park

Walk Overview: This loop route follows sidewalks and trails through the communities of Briar Hill, St. Andrews Heights and West Hillhurst. The portions of the walk along Toronto Crescent, in Shagnessey Heights Park and on the escarpment slope on the south side of Briar Hill have excellent views.
Length: 5.2 km
Route Description & Accessibility: This route does not have good accessibility. Some of the ascents/descents are steep and difficult to negotiate. The pedestrian overpass at Crowchild Trail and 14th Avenue has stairs but there are no accessible ramps on either end of the overpass. The narrow trails in Shagnessey Heights Park and the trail on the escarpment slope on the south side of Briar Hill both have poor accessibility. There are no detours listed in the text.
Food and Drink: There are benches and tables in Lions Park. Along the route you pass a gas station convenience store. Another option is to visit the

food court at the nearby North Hill Centre when you arrive back at the station.

Washrooms: There are no public washrooms along the route. At North Hill Centre the washrooms are next to the food court.

Map References: Clear-View – 27, MapArt – 154 & 153
Rand McNally – 48, Sherlock - 26

Route Category: Walk – The route starts and ends at the station (no bus is required)

The Walk: The starting point for the walk is at the west end of the south platform. Passengers arriving at the station on an eastbound Somerset-Bridlewood train walk to the back end of the platform. Passengers arriving on a westbound Crowfoot train walk to the track crossing at the front end of the platform and cross the tracks to the start of the walk.

From the west end of the south platform follow the path leading west through Lions Park to the traffic lights at 19th Street and 14th Avenue. Cross to the west side of 19th Street into the community of Briar Hill and walk west on 14th Avenue. The area occupied by Briar Hill was also once part of the large Riley family homestead. The land was annexed by the city in 1906 but residential development did not start until the 1950s. As you near the west end of 14th Avenue in Briar Hill the road goes down a short steep descent to a traffic wall separating 24th Street on the near side of the wall from Crowchild Trail on the far side of the wall. Use the nearby pedestrian overpass to reach the west side of Crowchild Trail (1.0 km). This overpass has stairs and no ramp.

From the west side of the overpass follow 13th Avenue on a more gradual descent to the traffic lights at University Drive. Cross University Drive into the community of St. Andrews Heights. The area occupied by this community was also part of the Riley family homestead. The city annexed the land in 1910. From 1912 to 1927 the public St. Andrews Golf Course occupied the land. The course became private at that time and continued to operate as a private course until the late 1940s. Residential development in St. Andrews Heights started in the 1950s.

On the right as you walk west one block from University Drive on 13th Avenue to Hamilton Street is the St. Andrews Community Park and Hall. At the north end of the park is an excellent toboggan hill. Of trivial interest is that there are five streets in the community named after Ontario cities (Toronto, Hamilton, Kingston, Windsor and London).

Turn left and walk south on Hamilton Street. After crossing 11th Avenue the street name changes to Toronto Crescent (1.5 km) and the road curves to the right heading west on the top edge of the escarpment in Shagnessey Heights Park. At this point a panoramic view opens up from downtown Calgary on your left to the mountains on your right. Keep walking along the grass on the south side of Toronto Crescent. Below you on the left are the partially treed slopes of Shagnessey Heights Park. The houses at the base of the escarpment are on the north edge of the community of Parkdale. The land for Parkdale was annexed by the city in 1910 with residential development starting in the late 1940s. There are a few older houses in the district that you will pass on Lions Park Walk 2 – Bow River Pathway – 29th Street to Shouldice Park.

After several blocks Toronto Crescent will begin to bend to the right. From here you can view the Foothills Hospital complex on the far side of 29th Street. Below you 29th Street angles across the escarpment slope down into Parkdale. Leave the edge of Toronto Crescent and turn left onto a dirt trail going down the slope (2.4 km). After a few steps downhill follow a trail to the left heading east into the trees. This trail remains flat until it emerges from the trees. Look for a very charming handmade bench along this trail. After leaving the trees angle to the right following a trail leading further down the slope towards the back of the houses on 7th Avenue. This trail continues east behind the houses all the way to the traffic wall on the west side of Crowchild Trail. Turn right and follow a paved path south keeping the traffic wall on your left. The path leads to the traffic lights at 5th Avenue and Crowchild Trail (3.5 km).

Cross to the east side of Crowchild Trail and head east on 5th Avenue in the community of West Hillhurst. The land for the West Hillhurst community

Bench in Shagnessey Heights Park

73

Shagnessey Heights Park slope looking southwest

was annexed by the city in 1907 although most of the development did not start until the mid 1940s. Today West Hillhurst is a mix of homes from the 1920s or earlier, homes from the mid-1940s or later and the more recent larger infills. In the first block of 5th Avenue you pass Grand Trunk Cottage School. This building and two other cottage schools in northwest Calgary are all that remain of seventeen cottage schools that were built in Calgary. At one time this district was known as Grand Trunk hence the name of the school.

Turn left at the end of the school field park and head north on 23rd Street to 7th Avenue. Make a right turn onto 7th Avenue and then make a left turn onto 22nd Street. At 9th Avenue turn right and walk one block east to where the road ends at the bottom southwest corner of another escarpment (4.3 km). On your left at the top of the escarpment are the houses on the south side of Briar Crescent in Briar Hill. From this corner of the escarpment follow a trail diagonally up the slope to the far northeast corner of the escarpment on the west side of 19th Street near 10th Avenue. When the trail ends at a sidewalk beside 19th Street turn left and continue a few more steps up a steep ascent to reach the top of the hill (4.7 km). Walk north on 19th Street to 14th Avenue and turn right following the path back through Lions Park to the station (5.2 km). Passengers catching an eastbound Somerset-

74

Bridlewood train use the near platform. Passengers catching a westbound Crowfoot train cross the tracks to the far platform.

Route Summary:

1. From the west end of the south platform follow a path west through Lions Park to the intersection of 19th Street and 14th Avenue.
2. Walk west on 14th Avenue to where a descent leads to the traffic wall beside Crowchild Trail.
3. Use the pedestrian overpass to reach the other side of Crowchild Trail.
4. From the west side of the overpass continue downhill on 13th Avenue and cross to the west side of University Drive at the traffic lights.
5. Continue west on 13th Avenue and turn left on Hamilton Street.
6. Walk south on Hamilton Street crossing 11th Avenue to where the street name changes to Toronto Crescent.
7. Follow Toronto Crescent south and then west along the top of the escarpment. Shagnessey Heights Park is on your left.
8. When Toronto Crescent begins to bend to the right turn left and follow a steep trail down the slope into Shagnessey Heights Park.
9. After a few steps turn left and follow a trail east into a treed area. This trail is reasonably flat until it emerges from the trees.
10. After leaving the trees angle to the right on a trail leading further down the slope towards the back of the houses on 7th Avenue.
11. Follow this trail behind the houses until you reach the traffic wall on the west side of Crowchild Trail.
12. Turn right and follow a path south beside the wall to the intersection of 5th Avenue and Crowchild Trail.
13. Cross Crowchild Trail and walk east on 5th Avenue.
14. Turn left on 23rd Street, then right on 7th Avenue and then left on 22nd Street.
15. At 9th Avenue turn right and walk east one block to the end of the road at the southwest corner of another escarpment slope.
16. Follow a trail diagonally up to the far northeast corner of the slope on the west side of 19th Street near 10th Avenue.
17. Turn left and follow 19th Street north to 14th Avenue.
18. Turn right and retrace your steps back through Lions Park to the station.

Lions Park Walk 2
Bow River Pathway –
29th Street to Shouldice Park

Walk Overview: For this walk you catch a bus to the start of this linear walk on the Bow River Pathway at 29th Street. The route heads west on the Bow River Pathway along the south side of Parkdale community. After passing to the south of Point McKay you walk by the south side of Montgomery before passing the end of Home Road as you enter Shouldice Athletic Park. The walk finishes near the northwest corner of Shouldice Park. A variety of birds and waterfowl can often be seen beside or on the river. From the end of the route you catch a bus back to the station.

Length: 5.7 km

Route Description & Accessibility: This mostly flat route has good accessibility. There is a short descent west of the Edworthy Park parking lot. At Home Road you have to take a few steps of descent/ascent where the two sections of pathway east and west of Home Road do not directly connect. In Shouldice Park there are a couple of crossings of a bumpy road. There is also a short descent/ascent as the path goes under Shouldice and James Hextall Bridges.

Food and Drink: There are picnic tables in Shouldice Park and benches in Lions Park. You pass two great coffee shops, a restaurant and an ice cream shop.

Washrooms: Along the route there is a washroom building at the north Edworthy Park parking lot and washrooms in the Shouldice Park picnic area and at the Shouldice Indoor Swimming Pool.

Map References: Clear-View – 26 & 16, MapArt – 153
Rand McNally – 47 & 37, Sherlock – 26, 25 & 17

Route Category: Bus/Walk/Bus – Ride the bus to the start of the route and when finished the walk ride the bus back to the station.

Bus Directions from the station to the start of the walk: Cross to the north side of 14th Avenue across from the station. Catch bus # 40 Crowfoot at stop 5735. Get off the bus at stop 5016 on westbound Parkdale Boulevard just west of 29th Street. This stop is 12 minutes from the station. The bus frequency is 35 minutes daily.

The Walk: After getting off the bus walk a few steps back to the traffic lights at Parkdale Boulevard and 29th Street. Cross to the south side of Parkdale Boulevard and walk straight ahead on a path that connects to the Bow River Pathway. The pathway is twinned in this area. Use caution crossing the bicycle path that is closer to the road. The walking path is closer to the river.

In the colder months walkers share the bike path with cyclists. This shared path is cleared of snow throughout the winter.

Of trivial interest is that the name of the road you just crossed changes several times. At Crowchild Trail the westbound Memorial Drive changes its name to Parkdale Boulevard. The name then changes from Parkdale Boulevard to 3rd Avenue at 32nd Street. At 37th Street the name becomes Bowness Road, a name the road keeps until 85th Street.

Turn right on the walking path and begin walking west. The Bow River is on your left. Across the river is the main Canadian Pacific Railway line to Vancouver. Trains have been traveling along the base of the Spruce Cliff and Wildwood escarpment on their way to and from Vancouver since the driving of the last spike at Craigellachie, B.C. in 1885. The Bow River Pathway on the south side of the river is at the base of the escarpment beside the tracks.

The flat treed area immediately across the river from 29th Street is Lawrey Gardens Natural Area. John Lawrey moved to Calgary in 1882 from England and after spending some time in California and British Columbia settled on this piece of land where he operated a very successful market garden. Access to his property was along a road beside the railway tracks. Lawrey's home was located at the top of the hill in the area that is now the community of Spruce Cliff. The Douglas Fir Trail extends along the escarpment slope above the railway tracks. This trail was constructed in the 1970s and upgraded in the 1990s. Continuing west you can see a large slide area on the escarpment where attempts have been made to try and stabilize the slope.

On the north side of Parkdale Boulevard west of 30th Street there are several older houses that date back to pre-1920. This group of houses and another group of houses on 37th Street were built many years before the rest of the community became fully developed.

The path will become quieter after you pass 32nd Street and the main road (now called 3rd Avenue) is further away from the path. The road beside the path from 32nd Street to 37th Street is Parkdale Boulevard. There is a small restaurant at the corner of Parkdale Boulevard and 3rd Avenue. If you need an ice cream break turn right at 34th Street and walk one block north to an ice cream shop on the north side of 3rd Avenue. The sidewalk stamp on the northeast corner at Parkdale Boulevard and 34th Steet reads Bowness Road. The sidewalk stamp on the next corner to the west reads Parkdale Boulevard.

At 37th Street turn right and walk north to view the four older brick houses in the 100 and 200 blocks (.9 km). Look west into the townhouse complex at McKay Road to view a small sandstone building located a few steps west of 37th Street. The townhouse complex has been developed around this building. The house's original owner, Alfred McKay, worked as a ferryman on the Bow River at the Centre Street crossing. MacKay Road (note the spelling

The former McKay House at Point McKay

change) in Montgomery community is also named for Alfred McKay. The area occupied by the townhouse complex was once the site of a drive-in theatre.

Retrace your steps south on 37th Street to the Bow River Pathway and turn right to continue walking west (1.4 km). At the west end of Point McKay a small access road (Shaganappi Way) leads south from the Bowness Road and Shaganappi Trail intersection to the north parking lot for Edworthy Park. On the west side of the parking lot is a charming little coffee shop. The Point McKay washroom building is on the east side of the parking lot. Harry Boothman pedestrian bridge, built in 1977, connects the north bank of the river to Edworthy Park on the south bank (2.7 km). Harry Boothman, the City of Calgary Parks Superintendent from 1961 to 1976, was a strong supporter of the trail and pathway system we now enjoy. An information plaque at the north end of the bridge provides information about Edworthy Park.

The land occupied by Edworthy Park was once part of the huge Cochrane Ranche property. Thomas Edworthy established his homestead called Shaganappi Ranch in the area of the present day park after receiving his land title in 1883. He operated a market garden using a spring on the escarpment as his water supply. Edworthy also operated a sandstone quarry. The city purchased the Edworthy property in the 1960s. At that time there were a couple of suggested uses for the property. One idea was to extend Shaganappi Trail across the river and up the hill to connect with Sarcee Trail. Another suggested use was to develop a sewage treatment plant in the area.

Looking across the river, we have to be thankful the natural beauty of Edworthy Park was preserved.

Continue walking west from the bridge. At Home Road the path continues west on the south side of Shouldice Athletic Park (3.6 km). Shouldice Park is 28 hectares in size. At the west end of the playing fields the path turns to the right away from the river and heads north to where the path ends at 13th Avenue. Cross to the north side of 13th Avenue and turn left walking west along the edge of the road. A large treed off-leash area is on the south side of 13th Avenue. At one time there was a mobile home park on this site. The path starts again near the west end of the athletic park. Cross the road as it goes under the 16th Avenue Bridge (5.1 km). On the north side of the bridge the road name changes to Monserrat Drive.

After crossing under the bridge follow the path north through the picnic area of Shouldice Park. James and Mary Shouldice settled in Calgary in 1901. In the 1910s, James and his neighbour Alfred McKay donated 100 acres to the city of Calgary for use as a park with the condition that the city would extend the street railway as far as the bridge that crosses the Bow River at the north end of Shouldice Park. The path through the picnic area goes under Shouldice Bridge constructed in the 1980s and the older steel James Hextall Bridge constructed in 1910/11. Starting in 1912 Calgarians could ride the streetcar across this older bridge on the way to and from Bowness Park. The older bridge has been preserved for the use of pedestrians and cyclists.

Climb stairs or a ramp to reach the deck of the James Hextall Bridge (5.5 km). One plaque partway across the bridge acknowledges James Hextall's

Tram en route to Bowness Park, ca. 1913-1919.
Glenbow Archives NA-4585-9

Along the Bow River Pathway near 37th Street NW

donation of the land for Bowness Park in exchange for the city extending the streetcar from the bridge west as far as Bowness. Another plaque mentions the Shouldice family. Unfortunately these plaques have become very faded and could use some restoration work.

From James Hextall Bridge walk east on the north side of Bowness Road and cross to the south side at 52nd Street at the pedestrian crossing light. Turn left after crossing Bowness Road and walk a few steps to the bus stop and the end of the route.

Bus Directions from the end of the route to the station:
Catch bus # 40 North Hill at stop 6639 on eastbound Bowness Road at 52nd Street. Get off the bus at stop 5735 on westbound 14th Avenue across the road from the station. The scheduled time back to the station is 24 minutes. The frequency of the bus is 35 minutes daily.

Route Summary:
1. From the station catch bus # 40 Crowfoot at stop 5735. Get off at stop 5016 on westbound Parkdale Boulevard at 29th Street.
2. Cross to the south side of Parkdale Boulevard at the traffic lights and walk straight ahead to reach the pedestrian path beside the river.
3. Turn right and walk west along the path to 37th Street.
4. Turn right and walk north on 37th Street to observe some older brick homes in the 100 and 200 blocks.

5. Retrace your steps on 37th Street back to the Bow River Pathway.
6. Continue west on the path to Home Road.
7. As you continue west from Home Road the path becomes joint use for walkers and cyclists.
8. Follow the path as it turns right away from the river and ends at 13th Avenue in Shouldice Athletic Park.
9. Turn left and walk west along 13th Avenue to where the path starts again on your right.
10. Follow the path as it crosses under the 16th Avenue Bridge and heads north through Shouldice Park.
11. The path leads under Shouldice Bridge and James Hextall Bridge.
12. Climb some stairs or a ramp to the deck of James Hextall Bridge.
13. From the bridge walk east to 52nd Street and cross to the south side of Bowness Road at the pedestrian crossing light.
14. Turn left and walk a few steps to stop 6639.
15. Catch bus # 40 North Hill and get off at stop 5735 on westbound 14th Avenue across from the station.

Lions Park Walk 3
Lions Park & Hounsfield Heights

Walk Overview: This short route wanders through Lions Park before making a loop through the community of Hounsfield Heights. The houses in this small community are south of Lions Park on the top of the escarpment and on the south-facing escarpment slope. The views towards the south along this route are excellent. There are a few older houses in the community.
Length: 3.0 km
Route Description & Accessibility: Portions of this route are relatively flat and accessible although there are some steep descents and ascents near the middle portion of the walk. There is no alternate route included the text.
Food and Drink: There are benches and tables in Lions Park. There are no stores, restaurants or coffee shops along the route. There is a food court at North Hill Centre.
Washrooms: There are no public washrooms along the route. The washrooms at North Hill Centre are next to the food court.
Map References: Clear-View – 27, MapArt – 154
Rand McNally – 49, Sherlock – 26
Route Category: Walk – The route starts and ends at the station (no bus is required)
The Walk: Passengers arriving at the station on an eastbound Somerset-Bridlewood train walk to the front end of the platform. Passengers arriving

on a westbound Crowfoot train walk to the back end of the platform and turn right crossing both sets of tracks to the start of the route. Use caution when crossing the tracks.

From here turn left and begin following the path east through Lions Park. Look for a large older house on the south side of the park. Near the east end of the park take a path to the right that exits the park onto 15th Street (0.5 km). Head south on 15th Street. This road becomes a steep downhill with cement stairs on both sides of the street. Turn right onto 10th Avenue and walk west one block turning right to head north on 16th Street. West of this area is an undeveloped green space. Follow 16th Street north to the south edge of Lions Park. Turn left and follow an alley west to where 16A Street meets 13th Avenue.

Turn left and walk south one block on 16A Street to 12th Avenue. From here follow an unpaved road on your right (17th Street) south and west behind the houses on the south side of 12th Avenue between 16A and 17A Streets (1.4 km). The road is at the top edge of an undeveloped green space with a good view to the south. Much of the undeveloped green space in Hounsfield Heights has underground water flow that limits where homes can be built. When this road ends at 17th Street turn right and walk north to 12th Avenue. Turn left and walk west on 12th Avenue to 18th Street. Again turn left and walk south on 18th Street making a right turn onto 11th Avenue (2.0 km). Walk west on 11th Avenue and turn right on 18A Street walking north back to 12th Avenue.

Turn right and follow 12th Avenue east back to 16A Street. Make a left turn onto 16A Street, retracing a short portion of your earlier route back to 13th Avenue. Turn left and walk west on 13th Avenue to 17A Street. Turn right and walk north between houses to where you re-enter Lions Park and walk a few steps to the left back to the station (3.0 km). Passengers catching an eastbound Somerset-Bridlewood train use the near platform. Passengers catching a westbound Crowfoot train cross the two sets of tracks to the far platform. Again use caution when crossing the tracks.

Route Summary:

1. From the south platform turn left and follow the path east through Lions Park to where a path on your right exits the park onto 15th Street.
2. Head downhill on 15th Street and turn right to go west on 10th Avenue.
3. Turn right and head north on 16th Street back to the edge of the park.
4. Turn left and follow an alley west to where 16A Street meets 13th Avenue.
5. Turn left and walk south one block on 16A Street.

Lions Park Station and The Renaissance condos

6. Follow an unpaved road on your right (17th Street) southwesterly from 16A Street to 17A Street.
7. Turn right and walk north on 17A Street to 12th Avenue.
8. Turn left and walk west on 12th Avenue.
9. Turn left again and walk south on 18th Street.
10. Turn right and walk west on 11th Avenue.
11. Turn right and walk north on 18A Street.
12. Turn right and walk east on 12th Avenue.
13. Turn left and walk north on 16A Street.
14. Turn left and walk west on 13th Avenue.
15. Turn right at 17A Street going north between houses to Lions Park.
16. Turn left and follow the path west back to the station.

Chapter Four
Banff Trail Station

Station Information: The station is located in a median between Capitol Hill Crescent on the east side and Banff Trail on the west side at 23rd Ave. The exits from the side platforms are at ground level. The track crossing is at the north end of the platforms. Use caution crossing the tracks. A pedestrian overpass across Crowchild Trail provides easy access to the parking lot beside McMahon Stadium. The platforms have unheated shelters.

The Banff Trail community on the east side of the station developed in the 1950s. The land had been annexed by the city in 1910. Motel Village is on the west side of the station. This area is a mix of hotels/motels, restaurants, small businesses and office buildings.

Banff Trail Walk 1
Banff Trail, Canmore Park & Collingwood

Walk Overview: The route passes through Banff Trail community before entering Canmore Park. You make a loop around the Confederation Park Golf Course and through the Collingwood community before crossing back through Canmore Park on the way back to the station. Many of the homes in the Capitol Hill community on the south side of the golf course were built in the 1950s although a few of the homes date back to the 1920s. In the past few years some new infill homes have been added to the community. Collingwood on the north side of the golf course is part of the residential area known as Triwood. The area was annexed by the city in 1910 although it did not develop as a residential community until some fifty years later. Along the route there are good views of the south slope of Nose Hill Park.

Length: 6.9 km

Route Description & Accessibility: This route has poor accessibility in several places. There are several steep descents/ascents spread throughout the route. The walking surface is a mix of sidewalks, paved paths, dirt trails and grass. One steep ascent is on grass. There are no alternate routes included in the text.

Food and Drink: There are tables and benches in Canmore Park. Along the route you pass a convenience store and a pizza take-out.

Washrooms: There are seasonal public washrooms beside the water park in Canmore Park.

Map References: Clear-View – 18, MapArt – 154
Rand McNally – 39, Sherlock – 26 & 18

Route Category: Walk – The route starts and ends at the station (no bus is required)

The Walk: The route starts at the north end of the two platforms on the east side of the tracks just south of 23rd Avenue on Capitol Hill Crescent. Cross over Capitol Hill Crescent and walk east on 23rd Avenue in Banff Trail. At 22nd Street turn left and walk north one block to 24th Avenue (0.5 km). Cross 24th Avenue and continue north on 22nd Street to Morley Trail. William Aberhart High School is on your left. In 1915, William Aberhart was appointed principal of Crescent Heights High School. He started broadcasting his *Back to the Bible Hour* program on CFCN radio in 1925. Aberhart also founded the Alberta Prophetic Bible Institute. As leader of the Social Credit Party, he served as Alberta premier from 1935 to 1943.

Of trivial interest is that four parallel roads in Banff Trail are named for locations between Calgary and Banff i.e. Exshaw, Morley, Cochrane and Canmore. In the south end of the community are two roads named Halifax and Victoria.

Turn left and walk northwest on Morley Trail and then turn right and walk northeast on 28th Avenue. Two short blocks will bring you to Canmore Road

Path in Canmore Park

and the south edge of the 15 hectares area of Canmore Park (1.3 km). Cross Canmore Road and turn right on the path walking southeast on the north side of the road. After one block the path angles to the left away from the road and descends in a northeasterly direction to a pedestrian crossing on 19th Street (1.8 km). The path on the east side of 19th Street turns to the right and goes south up a small ascent before turning left between the fence of Confederation Park Golf Course and a parking lot north of Holy Cross Anglican Church. Holy Cross is the former St. Cyprian's Anglican Church building. In 1997 when the congregation of St. Cyprian's amalgamated with the congregation of St. Michael and All Angels, the new name of Holy Cross was selected. St. Michael and All Angels Church opened in 1909 at 16th Avenue and 3rd Street NW. The church was enlarged in 1925 with additions in 1955 and 1957. The widening of 16th Avenue led to the closure of the church.

The path goes east past a playground and follows the golf course fence as it turns right and then left. The next section of the path heading east has a short steep descent quickly followed by a short steep ascent. For the first portion of this section an alley is on your right. The path then enters a narrow section between the golf course fence and the fence of a City of Calgary Maintenance Depot on your right. After turning right there is another descent/ascent as the path heads south before turning left and going east on the north side of 24th Avenue. In December this southeast corner of the golf course features the Lions Festival of Lights organized by the Lions from Calgary and area. Sponsors of the festival include Enmax, International Brotherhood of Electrical Workers, Sunshine Village Ski Resort, Calgary Herald, City of Calgary and Westburne Electric Supply.

Just before 14th Street the path splits (2.9 km). The path to the left goes through a tunnel under 14th Street into Confederation Park. The right branch turns left and passes over the tunnel entrance and heads north on the west side of 14th Street. Prior to the development of the golf course, the widening of 14th Street, and the development of the Rosemont community on the east side of 14th Street, there was a group of older houses in the 2700 block of 14th Street. When you reach the northeast corner of the golf course turn left and descend a switchback path into the south end of Collingwood. Walk west on the grass next to 31st Avenue beside the north fence of the golf course. The road then angles slightly to the right and changes its name to Constable Road.

When the road turns right and becomes Copithorne Road (4.2 km) leave the road and head west on a trail along the edge of the fence beside the golf course driving range. A short set of steps at the west end of the fence leads up to grass on the edge of Collingwood Drive. Turn left and follow the grass south past the entrance to the golf course parking lot. At 19th Street you cross over the road back into Canmore Park (4.6 km). Use caution here as

Misshapen trees in Canmore Park

there is no crosswalk. Walk straight ahead across the grass to a long row of trees. Look for a trail leading up to a main trail that crosses through the length of trees. Turn right and follow this trail to the west end of the treed area. There are picnic tables in this area.

When the path through the trees ends, angle to the right on the grass staying at the base of the slope on your left as you walk past the water park and a tennis court fence on your right. After passing the tennis courts keep walking straight ahead on the grass, crossing two paths that join partway up the slope on your left. Continue straight ahead to an area with trees that have trunks that are almost horizontal and somewhat misshapen. There are similar trees in Confederation Park just west of 10th Street. Keep the trees to your left as you pass through this area. The ground in the area near the trees is often wet.

After passing the trees continue straight ahead and ascend the steep slope to the east fence for the field of Banff Trail School. Walk a few steps to the left and enter the school field (5.2 km). Angle to the right across the field towards a natural area created by students, parents and staff of the school. The facilities here include a small seating area of large rocks and an aptly named short trail called Banff Trail that wanders through the natural area. There is also a plaque explaining how to tell time using your shadow.

Retrace your steps to the gateway and walk a few steps to your right to reach Canmore Road. Turn left and follow the path southeast beside Canmore Road to 28th Avenue. From here retrace your earlier route along 28th Avenue, Morley Trail, 22nd Street and 23rd Avenue back to the station (6.9 km). Use the near platform if you are catching a northbound Crowfoot train and the far platform if you are catching a southbound Somerset-Bridlewood train.

Route Summary:

1. The route starts at the north end of the two platforms on the east side of the tracks just south of 23rd Avenue on Capitol Hill Crescent.
2. Walk east on 23rd Avenue and turn left at 22nd Street.
3. Walk north on 22nd Street and turn left on Morley Trail.
4. Walk northwesterly on Morley Trail and turn right on 28th Avenue.
5. Walk northeasterly on 28th Avenue and cross Canmore Road to a path along the south side of Canmore Park.
6. Turn right and follow the path as it angles left away from the road and descends to a pedestrian crossing on 19th Street.
7. The path turns right with a short ascent and then turns left along the north side of a parking lot.
8. The path passes a playground as it follows beside the golf course fence turning right and then left.
9. The next section has a short steep descent quickly followed by a short steep ascent.
10. The path turns right heading south with a descent and an ascent before turning left along the north side of 24th Avenue near 15th Street.
11. When the path splits just before 14th Street take the right branch as it passes above the tunnel entrance and heads north beside 14th Street.
12. At the northeast corner of the golf course turn left and descend a switchback path to 31st Avenue.
13. Walk west beside the north fence of the golf course. The road's name changes to Constable Road.
14. When the road turns right you leave the edge of the road and continue west along the edge of the fence beside the golf course driving range.
15. A short set of steps leads you to the edge of Collingwood Drive.
16. Turn left and follow the golf course fence past the entrance to reach 19th Street.
17. Cross 19th Street back into Canmore Park.
18. Walk straight ahead across the grass to where a small trail leads to a main trail running lengthways through a long row of trees on top of a small rise.
19. Turn right and follow the trail west to the end of the trees.
20. From the end of the trees angle to the right along the base of a slope past the water park and the south side of tennis courts.

21. After the tennis courts keep walking straight ahead crossing two paths that join further up the slope on your left.
22. Continue across the grass keeping some misshapen trees on your left.
23. After the trees continue straight ahead climbing up a slope to the east fence of Banff Trail School field.
24. Turn left and walk a few steps to the gateway in the school fence.
25. Angle to your right across the field to a small natural area.
26. Retrace your steps to the gateway and turn right to reach the path beside Canmore Road.
27. Turn left and follow the path southeast back to 28th Avenue.
28. From here turn right and retrace your earlier route back to the station.

Banff Trail Station Walk 2
University Heights & West Campus Pond

Walk Overview: This loop route crosses to the west side of Crowchild Trail and wanders through Foothills Athletic Park on the north side of McMahon Stadium. You then pass through the University Heights community and make a circuit around West Campus Pond on the west side of the community. University Heights was developed in the 1960s. A walk along the quiet streets in this community beneath the many mature trees is very pleasant. From West Campus Park you have excellent views to the south and west. The final section of the route is on 24th Avenue NW along the north side of University Heights and Foothills Athletic Park.

Length: 5.6 km

Route Description & Accessibility: This is a relatively flat route with a mix of sidewalks, paved paths and dirt trails. A few sections of the route have poor accessibility. One short section is in a gravel back alley. The trail section at the south end of West Campus Pond can be difficult to negotiate due to the slant of the ground. Along the north side of University Heights the sidewalks do not have sloped curbs. No alternate routes are included in the text.

Food and Drink: There are benches by West Campus Pond. Stadium Shopping Centre has several restaurants and a bakery.

Washrooms: There are no public washrooms along this route.

Map References: Clear-View – 18 & 17, MapArt – 154 & 153
Rand McNally – 38 & 37, Sherlock – 26, 25, 17 & 18

Route Category: Walk – The route starts and ends at the station (no bus is required)

The Walk: The route starts at the north end of the two platforms on the west side of the tracks. Cross Banff Trail at the north end of the platforms and walk west a short distance on the sidewalk on the south side of 23rd Avenue at the north end of Motel Village. Use the pedestrian overpass to cross over Crowchild Trail.

On the west side of the overpass you are in the east side of the McMahon Stadium parking lot in Foothills Athletic Park. The stadium is the most prominent facility in the park. It was named for brothers Frank and George McMahon who made a $300,000 donation in 1960 to assist in the construction of the stadium. Construction of the stadium was completed in 100 days. The original seating for 22,000 has now been increased to over 35,000. The principal tenant of the stadium is the Calgary Stampeders Football Club. The Opening and Closing Ceremonies for the 1988 Winter Olympics were held in the stadium.

From the end of the pedestrian overpass ramp in the stadium parking lot, angle to your left towards the chain link fence on the north side of the parking lot. Turn left and walk along the edge of the parking lot towards the entrance to Foothills Stadium. This baseball stadium opened in 1966 and for a few years it was known as Burns Stadium. It was the home of the Calgary Vipers Baseball Club from 2004 until 2011. Other occupants have been the Calgary Expos Baseball Club from 1977 to 1984 and the Calgary Cannons Baseball Club from 1985 to 2002. The present capacity of the stadium is about 6,000.

As you continue further west Foothills Athletic Track is on the right. The Olympic Volunteer Centre, owned by the University of Calgary, is on the left at the north end of McMahon Stadium (0.6 km). The Red and White Club is located on the second floor. After passing the stadium follow along the edge of the athletic park fence to University Drive. There are several soccer fields in this section of the park. Turn right and follow the fence along the west side of the park to the traffic lights at University Drive and Unwin Road. Cross to the west side of University Drive and walk west on Unwin Road to Uxbridge Drive (1.3 km).

On your left at this corner is Stadium Shopping Centre. There is an interesting mix of shops and eating establishments in this small shopping centre. Cross to the west side of Uxbridge Drive and turn right. The first building on the left is Our Lady Queen of Peace Roman Catholic Church. The first building for this Polish congregation was dedicated in 1958 at 207 – 6th Ave SE in Riverside/Bridgeland. The congregation purchased their present property in 1962 with the present church building opening in 1968. The church has a very distinctive shape. On the lawn is a bust of John Paul II.

Uxbridge Drive makes a gradual turn to the left and heads west. You pass by the north side of Sir William Van Horne School. William Cornelius Van Horne was born in Illinois. After serving as the superintendent of the Chicago and Alton Railway, he became the general manager of the Canadian Pacific

Bust of Pope John Paul II

Railway in 1882. One of his duties was the supervision of the construction of the railway over the Rockies to Vancouver. He was appointed chairman and president of the company in 1888. Van Horne was recognized many years ago with the naming of Van Horne Avenue in the Connaught district although in 1904 city council decided to drop place names for many city streets in favour of numbered streets. Van Horne Avenue became 12th Avenue S.

At Uxbridge Drive and Urbana Road you pass Foothills Mennonite Church. A plaque on a rock dated 2006 recognizes the 50th anniversary of this congregation. The present building dates to the 1960s. At Uralta Road turn left and walk south to a large community park (1.9 km). Cross diagonally in a southwesterly direction across the park to Ungava Road. Follow Ungava Road south a short distance to Utah Drive and turn right. Make a left turn onto Umber Place. Turn right off Umber Place and follow a back alley west. Turn left through a gateway in a fence into a green space that extends east along the south side of the community to Stadium Shopping Centre.

Go right along the fence line passing through another gateway into the southeast corner of West Campus Pond Park (2.4 km). From here continue straight ahead on a trail up a short ascent to view the pond. From here there is an excellent view across Bow River valley towards southwest Calgary and the mountains. Turn left and follow a trail around the south and west side of the pond. The trail joins a path near West Campus Boulevard. Turn right on the path. At the first junction you turn right and walk down the path to benches that overlook the pond (2.9 km).

Return to the main path and continue to the next pathway junction. Turn left and walk north through the park. On the left are Ronald McDonald House and the Alberta Children's Hospital. At the next junction take the right branch to reach 24th Avenue (3.5 km). Turn right and follow 24th Avenue east along the north side of University Heights. The University of Calgary is on the left on the north side of 24th Avenue. At University Drive cross to the east side at the traffic lights to the corner in front of Father David Bauer Arena (4.4 km). Father Bauer was a Catholic priest who played a key role in the formation of a Canadian national hockey team in 1962. A second arena to the south is named for Norma Bush, a Calgary nurse, who was very active in sports and community activities. Norma's interests included the Calalta Figure Skating Club, fastball, basketball and hockey.

A path leads east on the south side of 24th Avenue past the north side of Foothills Athletic Park. You pass Foothills Indoor Pool, the Volleydome and Foothills Stadium. When you reach the traffic lights at Crowchild Trail cross to the southeast corner and angle right to follow Capitol Hill Crescent south to the station (5.6 km). On the right you pass the two entrances to the C-train tunnels under the intersection of 24th Avenue and Crowchild Trail. Catch the

West Campus Pond

northbound Crowfoot train on the near platform. Catch the southbound Somerset-Bridlewood train on the far platform.

Route Summary:

1. Cross Banff Trail on the west side of the station and walk straight ahead crossing the pedestrian overpass to the west side of Crowchild Trail.
2. From the end of the pedestrian overpass ramp, angle to the left towards a chain link fence along the north side of the parking lot.
3. Turn left and follow the fence past the entrance to Foothills Stadium, past the Olympic Volunteer Centre and past Foothills Athletic Track.
4. Continue to follow the fence past some soccer fields to reach University Drive.
5. Turn right and follow University Drive north to Unwin Road.
6. Cross University Drive and follow Unwin Road west to Uxbridge Drive.
7. Turn right and follow Uxbridge Drive north and then west to Uralta Road.
8. Turn left and walk south on Uralta Road to the northeast corner of a large community park.
9. Cross diagonally across the park to reach Ungava Road.
10. Follow Ungava Road south to Utah Drive and turn right.
11. Make a left turn onto Umber Place.
12. Turn right off Umber Place into an alley.
13. Walk through a gateway in the fence on the south side of the alley.
14. Turn right and walk through a second gateway into the southeast corner of West Campus Park.
15. Walk straight ahead up a slight ascent to where you can view the pond.
16. Turn left and follow a trail around the south and west sides of the pond until you reach a path beside West Campus Boulevard.
17. Turn right on this path taking the left branch at the first two junctions.
18. At the third junction take the right branch following the path north to 24th Avenue.
19. Turn right and follow 24th Avenue east crossing University Drive and Crowchild Trail.
20. From the southeast corner of 24th Avenue and Crowchild Trail turn right and follow Capitol Hill Crescent south to the station.

Chapter Five
University Station

Station Information: The station is located in the centre median of Crowchild Trail between 24th Avenue and 32nd Avenue/Charleswood Drive. When the Northwest line opened in 1987 this station was the terminus for the line. Pedestrian overpasses at the north end of the centre platform cross Crowchild Trail to the University campus to the west and to Banff Trail community to the east. The station building has an elevator and stairs leading up to the pedestrian overpasses. The station has no park and ride lots. Route # 20 Heritage/Northmount is the only bus route with stops close to the station on Campus Drive beside the Biological Sciences Building.

University Station is one of four northwest stations located in the centre median between the northwest bound and southeast bound traffic lanes of Crowchild Trail. Brentwood, Dalhousie and Crowfoot Stations are also located in the median. The new Tuscany Station scheduled to open in 2014 will also be in the centre median. Crowchild Trail is named for Tsuu T'ina chief David Crowchild (1899-1982).

In 1945 a Calgary branch of the University of Alberta opened. This branch gained autonomy in 1966 with the establishment of the University of Calgary. The two oldest buildings on the campus are the Administration Building and Science A Building constructed in 1960.

University Walk 1
Campus – Short Loop

Walk Overview: This route is a loop through the central part of the campus. On this walk you pass many of the main buildings on campus. There are several works of art along the route.

Length: 2.3 km

Route Description & Accessibility: Most of this relatively flat route has good accessibility. The walking surface is a mix of paved paths and sidewalks.

Food and Drink: MacEwan Student Centre has a large food court.

Washrooms: There are washrooms in the university buildings along the route.

Map References: Clear-View – 71, MapArt – 154 & 153 Rand McNally – 38, Sherlock – 45

Route Category: Walk – The route starts and ends at the station (no bus is required).

The Walk: From the upper level of the station turn left and cross the overpass to the west side of Crowchild Trail on the eastern edge of the campus. At the bottom of the stairs and/or ramp walk a few steps west to where a sidewalk junction offers three choices of route. The sidewalk to the right is the route for Walk 2. The sidewalk to the left is near the end of Walks 1 and 2. Take the middle sidewalk, walking to the pedestrian crossing on Campus Drive. On your left near the junction is an interesting looking sculpture entitled *Magyer Centennial Gateway*. The sculpture is dedicated to the Hungarian immigrants who chose to make Canada their home.

After crossing Campus Drive continue straight ahead on the sidewalk. On your left is a parking lot and on the right is the Biological Sciences Building. Cross a parking lot access road and follow the sidewalk as it passes under a pedestrian walkway connecting the Social Sciences Tower on your right to the Administration Building on your left. The tower constructed in 1969 houses the faculties of Communication and Culture, Humanities and Social Sciences. The Administration Building was one of the first two buildings constructed on the campus in 1960. The building was first known as the Arts and Education Building. The offices of the Department of Psychology and the office of the university president are located in this building. In the centre of the building is an atrium area with plants. Marble statues of Socrates and his pupils Plato and Krito add to the atmosphere of this pleasant area.

Continuing west on the sidewalk, the older building on your right is the Science A Building. This building is the second of the two oldest buildings on the campus. On the west side of the Administration Building is a large open green space known as Swann Mall. There are several sculptures in this area. Probably the most well known situated atop a small grassy knoll is *Untitled Steel Sculpture* by artist George Norris.

On the west side of Swann Mall is the MacKimmie Library Tower and Block Buildings. You will pass by the front of the library later in this walk. Start to angle to the right at the corner of the Science A Building heading towards an opening between the MacEwan Hall Building immediately north of the Library Block Building and the Science B Building to the right. An underground walkway connects these two buildings.

MacEwan Hall and the attached MacEwan Student Centre to the west are named for Grant MacEwan, former mayor of Calgary, Lieutenant Governor of Alberta, and author of many books on Western Canadian history. The Student Centre was constructed just prior to the 1988 Winter Olympics. As you pass by the south side of the Science B Building take a moment to step inside the entrance door to view a group of sandstone gargoyles that were originally on the Calgary Herald Building at 7th Avenue and 1st Street SW. More of these gargoyles are in Colonel Walker Park, a small park at the +15

Gargoyles in Science B Building

level on 7th Avenue adjacent to 1st Street West CTrain Station.

After passing between the buildings angle to the left along the north side of MacEwan Hall. On your right is the former Nickle Arts Museum Building opened in 1979, thanks to a $1 million donation by oilman Sam Nickle. The museum is now in the Taylor Family Digital Library that you will pass later in this route.

From the Museum Building, keep to the left following the sidewalk on the north side of the MacEwan Student Centre Building (0.6 km). To your right on the north side of Collegiate Boulevard is the Engineering Building. Continue walking west on the sidewalk beside Collegiate Boulevard. After passing a small parking lot on the left adjacent to the Kinesiology Building follow the sidewalk leading away to the left from Collegiate Boulevard. This sidewalk leads to an enclosed walkway connecting the Kinesiology Building to the Olympic Oval (1.0 km). Just north of the entrance to the walkway are several points of interest.

A large red sculpture entitled *Spire* by artist Bob Boyce represents human movement – crawling, walking, running, jumping and flying. Before walking underneath the sculpture stop and look at the Olympic Cauldron. The Oval was one of the host sites for the 1988 Winter Olympics. Walking south towards the entry doors to the walkway there is a group of trees on the left.

Dated plaques indicate the year that each tree was placed in this area. On the right are plaques with information about the Oval.

Upon entering the Oval look for several display cases with information and displays about the Olympics. The admission kiosk for the Oval is to your right on the main level. There is a nominal fee to enter the Oval. Stairs lead up to more display cases on the second level. Along the hallway on the left in the Kinesiology Building there are numerous display cases of photos and memorabilia for various university teams and athletes. If the blinds are open on the left side of the hallway you can view the Jack Simpson Gymnasium. Beyond the gymnasium is the Fitness and Lifestyle Centre. On the right along this hallway is the entrance to the Outdoor Centre (complete with a climbing wall) and the Racquet Centre.

At the top of the stairs in the enclosed walkway for the Oval are two glass art pieces entitled *Pagoglyths (Marks on Ice)* by Brian Baxter. They depict the marks a skater leaves on a clear ice surface. Return back down the stairs and exit the walkway on the south side. Above these doors is a bronze frieze entitled *Brothers of the Wind* by Robert McKenzie. This 1925 sculpture was originally created for the Philadelphia Skating Club. To your right as you follow the sidewalk away from the entry doors is a metal sculpture entitled *La Patineur de Vitesse '84 (The Speed Skater)* by artist Germain Bergeron. The sculpture is a tribute to Canadian speed skater Gaetan Boucher, winner of two gold medals and one bronze medal at the 1984 Winter Olympics.

At the southwest corner of the Kinesiology Building turn left and follow the sidewalk along the south side of the building beside University Court. The Dining Centre Building is on the right as you turn at the southwest corner of the Kinesiology Building with the residence buildings to the south and west of the Dining Centre. On your right as you follow University Court is one of the newer campus buildings (Hotel Alma or International House). University Gate (an access road leading to 24th Avenue) separates Hotel Alma from the Rozsa Centre (opened in 1997). The Reeve Theatre and the University Theatre buildings are connected to the Rozsa Centre.

At the southeast corner of the Kinesiology Building the route angles to the left towards the south side of the MacEwan Student Centre. Walk towards a large arched metal sculpture entitled *Olympic Arch* by artists Colette Whiten and Paul Kipps. This arch, supported by eight bronze figures, was the official entrance to the Athletes Village during the 1988 Olympic Winter Games. After the Olympics the sculpture was moved downtown for a couple of years and placed in front of the Municipal Building. In 1991 the sculpture was moved to this location to commemorate the 25th anniversary of University of Calgary. Look for a bright red and yellow sculpture of a dinosaur to the left of the arch near the east entry doors to the Kinesiology Building. The university sports teams are known as the Dinos.

From the arch continue walk east along the north side of University Court road. After passing the MacEwan Student Centre on your left you will pass between MacEwan Hall on your left and the Taylor Family Digital Library on your right. Calgary philanthropists Don and Ruth Taylor donated $25 million towards the construction of the library. At the northwest corner of Swann Mall make a right turn passing the front doors of the MacKimmie Library Building (1.7 km). Ross MacKimmie served three terms as Chair of the university's Board of Governors. Walk south through the open park area of the mall to where there is a slight rise as you cross above an underground walkway connecting the Murray Fraser Hall (1994) on your right to the Professional Faculties Building on your left. These two buildings are home to the Law, Nursing, Social Work and Environmental Design Faculties. Murray Fraser was president and vice-chancellor of the university from 1988 to 1996. University Way just south of this location is the major bus stop area for the university.

The route turns left and heads east along the south side of the Professional Faculties Building passing under an elevated walkway connecting this building to the Education Complex and Tower Buildings on your right. The Education Tower is in turn connected by an elevated walkway to the Scurfield Hall Building that houses the Haskayne School of Business. Ralph Scurfield was a Calgary businessman and philanthropist. The school of business, named after Richard Haskayne, was founded in 1967. At the southeast corner of the Professional Faculties Building follow a sidewalk that angles to the left towards a smaller building (the Child Care Centre) on the west side of Campus Drive. After passing this building cross Campus Drive and follow the sidewalk back past the gateway sculpture to the University Station overpass (2.3 km).

Swann Mall on University of Calgary campus

Route Summary:

1. At the upper level of the station turn left and cross the pedestrian overpass to the west side of Crowchild Trail.
2. Follow the sidewalk west until it splits in three.
3. Take the centre branch, cross Campus Drive and continue straight ahead.
4. Cross an access road and then walk under the pedestrian walkway between the Social Sciences Tower on your right and the Administration Building on your left.
5. Continue straight ahead and angle to the right as you pass the corner of the Science A Building.
6. Head for the opening between the MacEwan Hall Building on your left and Science B Building on your right.
7. After passing between the buildings angle to the left keeping MacEwan Hall to your left.
8. Continue to follow the sidewalk along the north side of MacEwan Student Centre Building. Collegiate Boulevard is on your right.
9. After passing a small parking lot angle to the left and follow the sidewalk leading to the north doors of the enclosed walkway between the Kinesiology Building and the Olympic Oval.
10. Exit the walkway by the south doors and walk south.
11. Turn left at the southwest corner of the Kinesiology Building. Hotel Alma or International House is on your right.
12. At the southeast corner of the Kinesiology Building angle to the left towards the south side of the MacEwan Student Centre.
13. Continue walking east keeping MacEwan Student Centre and then MacEwan Hall on your left and the Taylor Family Digital Library on your right.
14. Make a right turn at the northeast corner of the MacKimmie Library Building.
15. Walk to the south end of Swann Mall and turn left.
16. Walk under an elevated pedestrian walkway between the Professional Faculties Building on your left and the Education Tower on your right.
17. At the southeast corner of the Professional Faculties Building angle to the left following a sidewalk towards a smaller building (the Child Care Centre).
18. Cross Campus Drive and continue on the sidewalk past the first junction after you left the station.

University Walk 2
Campus – Long Loop

Walk Overview: This route makes a larger loop than the previous route along the outer edge of the campus.

Length: 4.5 km

Route Description & Accessibility: This relatively flat route has good accessibility. The walking surface is a mix of paved paths, sidewalks and grass. You may have to detour on paved paths near the end of the route to avoid a section on grass.

Food and Drink: MacEwan Student Centre has a large food court.

Washrooms: There are washrooms along the route in the campus buildings.

Map References: Clear-View – 71, MapArt – 154 & 153
Rand McNally – 38 & 37, Sherlock – 45

Route Category: Walk – The route starts and ends at the station (no bus is required).

The Walk: The route starts at the bottom of the ramp and/or stairs on the west side of Crowchild Trail. The sidewalk leads west away from the road. In a few steps the sidewalk reaches a junction with three options. Take the sidewalk angling to the right. The left sidewalk at the junction is on the route near the end of both Walks 1 and 2. The centre sidewalk at the junction is at the start of Walk 1. In a few steps from the junction you reach a pedestrian crosswalk for Campus Drive. The Biological Sciences building is on the other side of the crosswalk. Do not cross the road here. Continue following the sidewalk as it crosses through a treed area to another junction beside 32nd Avenue (0.4 km).

Turn left and follow the path west past the north side of the EEEL (Energy, Environment, Experiential Learning) Building. This building opened in the fall of 2011. When the path reaches the traffic lights at 32nd Avenue and Campus Drive cross to the west side of Campus Drive. On the left is a large campus map. The building directly south of the intersection is the ICT (Information and Communications Technologies) Building. This building, constructed in 2001, is the home to the offices of the Departments of Computer Science and Computer & Electrical Engineering.

From the west side of Campus Drive continue west along the path. On your left is the Engineering Building. The path continues west past the CCIT (Calgary Centre for Innovative Technology) Building. This building opened in 2002 as a research facility for engineering, science, medicine and kinesiology. In this area the path has a section with a small ascent. As you pass a large parking lot on the left the path descends to a set of lights at a T-intersection for 32nd Avenue and Collegiate Boulevard (1.1 km). Cross to the

Community garden on University of Calgary campus

west side of Collegiate Boulevard and continue westbound on the path. There is another large parking lot on your left. On the north side of 32nd Avenue there is Varsity Fire Station # 17.

When the path splits take the left branch. The path leads to Varley Drive on the north side of Varsity Courts student housing. Keep to the edge of the road or use the sidewalk beside Varsity Courts as you continue westbound to where the path starts again just before the intersection of 39th Street and 32nd Avenue (1.6 km). Turn left and follow the path south along the west side of 39th Street. You will cross the entry road into Varsity Courts. There is a short ascent along this section of path.

At a T-intersection use the crosswalk to reach the south side of the road. West Campus Way is the road to your right. You can see the Alberta Children's Hospital to your right. Collegiate Road is the road to the left. Turn left and follow the path to an access road. A community garden is on the north side of Collegiate Road. Cross the access road and turn right walking south on the east side of the access road. There are playing fields on both sides of the access road and sidewalk. On your right as you near 24th Avenue is the Physical Plant building (2.6 km). South of this building is the Child Development Centre building. Look for the large decorative handprint on the east wall. Turn left and follow the sidewalk east along the south side of the

Magyer Centennial Gateway

campus on the north side of 24th Avenue. The Banff Trail Walk 2 route is on the south side of 24th Avenue. Continue east past the Heating Plant building on your left. Walk past the student residences. After passing the last residence, Cascade Hall, cross University Gate.

Continue east on 24th Avenue with the Art Building and Parkade on the left. At the major intersection on the south side of the campus where University Drive meets 24th Avenue (3.5 km), cross the road at the traffic lights and continue east along the north side of 24th Avenue. At the next access road (Campus Gate) cross to the east side of the road and turn left following the path north to an intersection with Campus Drive. Turn right and continue on the path beside Campus Drive. On the far side of Campus Drive is Scurfield Hall on the right with the Education Tower & the Education Classroom buildings to the left on the west side of Scurfield Hall.

The path ends as you reach the last parking lot access road on the right hand side of Campus Drive. Cross the access road and continue walking beside Campus Drive on the grass. If you require better accessibility than the grass cross Campus Drive and follow sidewalks to reach the Child Care Centre Building. As you pass the Child Care Centre Building on the other side of Campus Drive follow a sidewalk angling to the right to reach the overpass leading to the station (4.5 km).

Route Summary:

1. At the upper level of the station turn left and cross the pedestrian overpass to the west side of Crowchild Trail.
2. Follow the sidewalk west until it splits in three.
3. Take the sidewalk to the right angling towards Campus Drive.
4. Stay on the same side of Campus Drive following the sidewalk through a treed area to another junction beside 32nd Avenue.
5. Turn left and follow the path west past the north side of the EEEL (Energy, Environment, Experiential Learning) Building.
6. At the traffic lights cross to the west side of Campus Drive and continue west on the path with 32nd Avenue on your right.
7. At the traffic lights at Collegiate Boulevard cross to the west side and continue westbound.
8. Walk past the north side of Varsity Courts and turn left at 39th Street.
9. Walk south on 39th Street and use the crosswalk to reach the south side of the road with West Campus Way on your right and Collegiate Road on your left.
10. Turn left and then turn right following a path south with playing fields on your left and right and an access road on your right.
11. At 24th Avenue turn left and follow the path east along the south side of the campus.
12. Continue on this path crossing several access roads until you reach University Drive.
13. Cross University Drive and continue east on the path.
14. At Campus Gate cross to the far side and turn left following the path north to Campus Drive.
15. Turn right and follow the path beside Campus Drive until the path ends.
16. Continue on the grass beside the road until you reach a sidewalk angling to the right towards the station. This sidewalk was also at the end of Walk 1.
17. Follow the sidewalk back to the station.

Chapter Six
Brentwood Station

Station Information: Brentwood Station is located in the median of Crowchild Trail just east of 40th Avenue and Brisebois Drive. Brentwood Station opened in 1990 as the first extension on the original Northwest line. Pedestrian overpasses at the east end of the centre platform cross to the south and north sides of Crowchild Trail. The station has stairs, an elevator and an escalator to access the overpasses. The far end of the north overpass has stairs and a ramp. The far end of the south overpass has stairs, a ramp and an elevator. A large park and ride lot and numerous bus stops are on the south side of Crowchild Trail. There are also several bus stops on the north side of Crowchild Trail. The station has a heated waiting area.

University Research Park on the south side of Crowchild Trail is a large complex of research and technological buildings to the north of the University of Calgary. To the west of the research park is the east end of Varsity Acres. Brentwood Co-op Centre and the Brentwood Village shopping complex are on the north side of Crowchild Trail. Brentwood Road runs parallel to Crowchild Trail from Charleswood Drive to Brisebois Drive. The development of the communities of Brentwood and Varsity Acres began in the early 1960s. Nose Hill Park to the north of Brentwood is one of Canada's largest urban parks.

Brentwood Walk 1
Research Park & Varsity Acres

Walk Overview: After leaving the station this route passes through Research Park, a small park with a pond where you may have the opportunity to view waterfowl. From the park the route makes a loop through the east part of Varsity Village in Varsity Acres before returning to Research Park on the way back to the station. The route has an out-and-back section from the station to Research Park.

Length: 3.7 km

Route Description & Accessibility: This relatively flat route has good accessibility on paved paths and sidewalks with short sections on trails or grass.

Food and Drink: Research Park has benches beside the pond. There are no stores or restaurants along this route. There is a grocery store and several restaurants on the north side of Crowchild Trail near the station.

Washrooms: There are no public washrooms along the route.

Map References: Clear-View – 17, MapArt – 153
Rand McNally – 38 & 37, Sherlock – 18 & 17

Route Category: Walk – The route starts and ends at the station (no bus is required)

The Walk: After exiting the station doors at the upper level turn right and cross the overpass above Crowchild Trail. Take the first set of stairs down to the bus stop area. Walk along the sidewalk past the bus stops and follow the station access road to 40th Avenue.

Turn left on 40th Avenue and at the traffic lights at 36th Street turn left. On your right on 36th Street is a parking lot for Research Park (0.7 km). A paved path loops around the small pond in the park. There are benches facing the water and a small roofed shelter at the southeast corner of the pond. On the north side of the pond is a fountain with water bursting forth and flowing down into the pond. Around the edge of the pond are some exercise stations. A playground is near the southwest corner of the park. Waterfowl are attracted to this area during the warmer months of the year. Some can be quite bold in seeking food handouts from park visitors. In the colder months of the year the pond is drained.

Follow the trail around the north side of the pond to the northwest corner where 37th Street meets 40th Avenue. Cross to the west side of 37th Street and turn left. Walk south and when you reach the second path leading to the right between the houses (1.0 km), turn right and follow this path west. The path will lead you to a large park with mature trees and playing fields on the east side of the former Jerry Potts School now occupied by Ecole Francophone du Nord-Ouest. Starting in 1874 Jerry Potts worked as a guide and interpreter for the NWMP for twenty-two years. He was descended from a Scottish father and a First Nations mother.

At the west end of the park you pass by the playing fields for the school. Continue straight ahead and turn left at 42nd Street. Walk south past the front of the school (1.7 km). Turn left and head east on a path along the south side of the park. At the southeast corner of the park continue east on the sidewalk between the houses. The route crosses Varsville Place before reaching 37th Street (2.5 km). Turn left and walk north back to the corner of 37th Street and 40th Avenue. Turn right and cross to the east side of 37th Street. Turn right and follow the remainder of the trail around the pond back to your starting point by the parking lot (3.7 km).

Route Summary:

1. From the upper level of the station turn right and cross the overpass

Research Park

above Crowchild Trail to the first set of stairs.
2. Walk down the stairs, turn right along the sidewalk past the bus stops and follow the station access road to 40th Avenue.
3. Turn left walking along 40th Avenue to the traffic lights at 36th Street and turn left.
4. Turn right into Research Park and follow the trail around the north side of the pond to the northwest corner by 37th Street and 40th Avenue.
5. Cross to the west side of 37th Street and turn left.
6. Walk south and take the second path to the right between the houses.
7. Follow the path until you reach the playing fields east of Jerry Potts School.
8. Keep walking straight ahead, turn left on 42nd Street and walk past the front of the school.
9. Turn left and follow the path along the south edge of the park.
10. Stay on the path crossing Varsville Place before you reach 37th Street.
11. Turn left and walk north on 37th Street back to 40th Avenue.
12. Cross to the east side of 37th Street.
13. Turn right and follow the trail around the west and south sides of the pond back to the parking lot.

Brentwood Walk 2
Nose Hill Park (Many Owls Valley)
& Whispering Woods

Walk Overview: This route begins and ends with linear sections joined to an out-and-back section in the middle. In the early portion of this walk you climb up the escarpment near the southwest corner of Nose Hill Park. Nose Hill Park with an area of 1129 hectares is one of the city's largest parks. After a tour of the Many Owls area in the park, the route follows the John Laurie Pathway to Dr. E.W. Coffin Elementary School and Whispering Woods, a natural area on the west side of the school. The city's Adopt-A-Park program has enabled the school and community to preserve this area. A series of trails and interpretive signs through the natural area provides a learning experience for the students and an enjoyable location for walkers.

Length: 6.8 km

Route Description & Accessibility: The long and steep out-and-back section in Nose Hill Park restricts the accessibility for this route. There are several other smaller hills along the route. No alternate routes are included in the text. The walking surface is a mix of sidewalks, paved paths and trails.

Food and Drink: There are no stores or restaurants along this route. There is a grocery store and several restaurants near the station.

Washrooms: There is a pit toilet building beside the Many Owls Valley parking lot at John Laurie Boulevard and Brisebois Drive.

Map References: Clear-View – 10, MapArt – 143 & 144
Rand McNally – 26, Sherlock – 18 & 17

Route Category: Bus/Walk/Bus – Ride the bus to the start of the route and when the walk is finished ride the bus back to the station.

Bus Directions from the station to the start of the walk: At the upper level of the station turn right and cross the pedestrian overpass above Crowchild Trail. Go down the first set of stairs. Catch bus # 143 Northwest Loop at stop 6846. Get off at stop 8996 on westbound 52nd Avenue just west of Brisebois Drive. This stop is 7 minutes from the station. The bus frequency is 30 minutes during mid-day on weekdays and 45 minutes on Saturday and Sunday.

The Walk: After getting off the bus turn right and walk the few steps back to Brisebois Drive. Turn left and walk uphill on Brisebois Drive to a pedestrian crosswalk just south of John Laurie Boulevard. Cross to the east side of Brisebois Drive and walk eastbound up an ascent on John Laurie Pathway. Take the path leading to the left to reach the *Whispering Grass Walkway* (0.6 Km). Students from Dr. Coffin School chose the name of this pedestrian overpass above John Laurie Boulevard leading into the Many

Whispering Grass Pathway across John Laurie Boulevard

Owls Valley area of Nose Hill Park. At each end of the overpass are two curved steel panels sculpted by Canmore artist Tony Bloom.

John Laurie moved to Calgary from Ontario in 1920 and began a long teaching career from 1923 to 1956. He taught at Western Canada College and Crescent Heights High School. Laurie was dedicated to the task of improving the life of Alberta's First Nations. A plaque honouring Laurie is beside the Many Owls Valley parking lot. There is more information on Nose Hill Park included with Sunnyside Walk 6 – Rubbing Stone Hill.

After crossing the overpass continue on the path to a junction (0.9 km). The left branch leads downhill to the parking lot and a pit-toilet washroom building. The route turns right at the junction and begins a long uphill climb as the path winds its way to the top of the hill. This is an excellent area for wildflowers in the spring and summer so perhaps bring your flower guidebook on this walk.

When the path reaches the flat top of the hill it continues along the top of the escarpment heading in a northwesterly direction until the path makes a sharp left turn at a junction (2.7 km). Dalhousie Walk 6 – Nose Hill Park - Meadowlark Prairie following a southeasterly direction also arrives at this junction. There are dirt trails leading roughly east and north from the junction. Retrace your steps from the junction back along the top of the

Many Owls Valley Trail looking southwest

escarpment, down the hill, across the overpass and back along the path to Brisebois Drive (5.1 km).

Cross to the west side of Brisebois Drive and continue west on the path behind the houses on the south side of John Laurie Boulevard. At Brenner Drive turn left back into Brentwood community (5.7 km). The first intersection is at the northeast corner of the Dr. E.W. Coffin School field. Ernest William Coffin came west to Calgary from Prince Edward Island in 1909 and served as principal of the Calgary Normal School from 1911 to 1940. For many years he was a member of the Senate of the University of Alberta and served on curriculum committees for the Department of Education. He also found time to be involved with the Home and School Association and in church activities.

Walk along the outside of the north school fence beside Brenner Drive to the Whispering Woods sign (5.9 km). A website has been created for this natural area. The trail system and information plaques located in this natural area were the result of the hard work of the parents, students and teachers at the school. Spend some time exploring the area before stopping to look at the natural area amphitheatre backing onto the west school fence. From there enter the school grounds and walk towards the school building to a series of brick planters surrounding a crafted sundial. This area was created to commemorate the 20th anniversary of the construction of the second school building on this site in 1975. The original building was destroyed by fire in 1974.

From this area walk around the south or right hand side of the school and past the parking lot to Barrett Drive (6.5 km). Turn right and follow Barrett Drive south downhill to where it ends at 52nd Avenue beside Barrett Park. Cross to the south side of 52nd Avenue at the end of the route (6.8 km).

Bus Directions from the end of the walk to the station:

Catch bus # 43 Northwest Loop at stop 7074 on eastbound 52nd Avenue near 33rd street. Get off the bus at stop 3845 back at the station. The scheduled time back to the station is 8 minutes. The bus frequency is 30 minutes during mid-day on weekdays and 45 minutes on Saturdays and Sundays.

Route Summary:

1. From the upper level of the station turn right and cross the pedestrian overpass to the south side of Crowchild Trail.
2. Catch bus # 143 Northwest Loop at stop 6846 and get off at stop 7062 on westbound 52nd Avenue at Brisebois Drive.
3. After getting off the bus walk the few steps back to Brisebois Drive.
4. Turn left and walk uphill on Brisebois Drive to a pedestrian crossing.
5. Cross to the east side of Brisebois Drive and walk eastbound up an ascent on John Laurie Pathway.
6. Take the path leading left to Whispering Grass Walkway.
7. Cross the overpass above John Laurie Boulevard into Nose Hill Park.
8. Follow the path on the far side of the overpass to a junction.
9. Turn right and follow the path as it climbs the slope.
10. From the top of the slope follow the path north until it makes a sharp left turn.
11. From here retrace your route back to the crosswalk on Brisebois Drive.
12. Cross to the west side of Brisebois Drive and continue west on the path to Brenner Drive.
13. Turn left and follow Brenner Drive past the north school fence to the Whispering Woods sign.
14. Explore the trails in Whispering Woods and then walk through the gateway on the west side of the school grounds.
15. Walk towards the brick planters west of the school and then walk around the south side (right) of the school to reach Barrett Drive.
16. Turn right and follow Barrett Drive south on a descent to 52nd Avenue.
17. Cross to the south side of 52nd Avenue and catch bus # 43 at stop 7074.
18. Get off at stop 3845 back at the station.

Brentwood Walk 3
Brentwood Murals

Walk Overview: This loop route wanders through Brentwood passing three community murals. Two of the murals are on the sides of commercial buildings and the third is in the lobby of Nose Hill Library.

Length: 5.2 km

Route Description & Accessibility: This relatively flat accessible route follows sidewalks and paved paths.

Food & Drink: There is a grocery store and several restaurants near the station, Along the route you pass a convenience store, a coffee shop, restaurants and a bakery.

Washrooms: The only public washrooms are in Nose Hill Library.

Map References: Clear-View – 10, MapArt – 153 & 154
Rand McNally – 38, Sherlock – 18 & 17

Route Category: Walk – The route starts and ends at the station (no bus is required).

The Walk: From the upper level of the station turn left and walk across the pedestrian overpass to the north side of Brentwood Road. At the bottom of the stairs turn left and head west past the bus stops on the north side of the road. The Brentwood Co-op Centre is on your right. When Brentwood Road meets Blakiston Drive turn right and follow a paved path that cuts diagonally across Blakiston Park. The back of the Co-op Store is on your right and several apartment buildings are on the left.

When the path ends at Blakiston Drive turn right and then left onto Bell Street. At Brentwood Boulevard (0.8 km) turn right and head east behind the Brentwood Village Shopping Centre to Charleswood Drive. At Charleswood Drive turn left and walk north to the traffic lights at Northmount Drive.

The first of the three community murals is located on the east side of the commercial building on the southwest corner of Northmount Drive and Charleswood Drive (1.8 km). Senator Patrick Burns School is across Charleswood Drive from this building. This mural, designed by Aaron Petruic, was finished in the summer of 2005. The mural shows some neighbourhood landmarks and activities with mountains in the background. Numerous youth volunteers assisted with the painting of the mural. Below the mural are the names of the design artist, the painters and project partners and sponsors.

Turn left and start heading west on Northmount Drive. You pass St. Luke's School and Brentwood School. Syrian-born St. Luke was a follower of St. Paul. Luke authored the Third Gospel and the Acts of the Apostles. On the

William Bruce Farm, 1894. Glenbow Archives NA-1097-1. This photo was probably taken looking north from near the vicinity of Brentwood Mall

west side of Brentwood School is a small natural area called *Green Garden*. To walk through the garden area turn left on the east side of the school and walk south and turn right along the south side of the school. A set of stepping stones leads through the garden area by the southwest corner of the school. From the west side of the garden turn right and walk north in an alley on the west side of the school. At Northmount Drive turn left and walk west to Brisebois Drive (2.8 km).

The second of the three community murals is located on the side of a commercial building on the northeast corner of Northmount Drive and Brisebois Drive. The view depicted on the mural is looking east with the skyline of downtown and local natural areas being depicted. Cheri Macaulay, an artist in the community, designed the mural that was finished in 2004. Again local young people assisted with the painting.

Continue walking west on Northmount Drive. As the road makes a gradual turn to the left you pass Captain John Palliser School. From 1857 to 1860 John Palliser led a scientific expedition through Western Canada exploring the area from Cypress Hills to the Rocky Mountains. From his explorations, Palliser came to the conclusion that very little would grow in southwest Saskatchewan and southeast Alberta, an area that came to be known as

Mural at Nose Hill Library just inside the entry doors

Palliser's Triangle. There are several small murals on the south wall of the school and a small natural area by the southeast corner of the school.

On the west side of the school are tennis courts next to the Sir Winston Churchill Pool and Sports Complex operated by the City of Calgary. North of the complex is the Brentwood Sportsplex (indoor arena). Turn right after passing the tennis courts and walk north to the front doors of Nose Hill Library (3.7 km). The third of the three murals is on the wall in the entryway of the library. Kirsten Horel, a local artist, designed this mural. Cheri Macaulay assisted Kirsten with the painting. This mural depicts the community in much more detail with information about the mural on a pillar inside the library.

The schools in Brentwood are considering the idea of creating a large mural on the north wall of the arena. After visiting the library cross to the south side of Northmount Drive at the pedestrian crosswalk. Turn right and walk west to Boulton Road and make a left turn. The small strip mall on the west side of Boulton Road has a coffee shop, a bakery and several other stores. Follow Boulton Road as it leads you south and then southeast to an intersection with Bulyea Road. Turn right and follow Bulyea Road one block southwest to Brentwood Green (4.3 km).

Turn left on Brentwood Green and walk to the end of the road where you follow a sidewalk a few steps past a traffic barrier wall to reach Brisebois

Drive. Cross Brisebois Drive and head east on Brentwood Road to the path you followed through Blakiston Park at the start of the walk. Rocky Mountain College is on your right. From the path retrace your steps back to the pedestrian overpass leading to the station (5.2 km).

Route Summary:

1. From the upper level of the station turn left and walk across the pedestrian overpass to the north side of Brentwood Boulevard.
2. At the bottom of the stairs, head west past the bus stops on the north side of the road.
3. Turn right on Blakiston Drive and then follow a path that cuts diagonally across Blakiston Park.
4. When the path ends at Blakiston Drive, turn right and then left onto Bell Street.
5. At Brentwood Boulevard turn right and walk east to Charleswood Drive.
6. Turn left on Charleswood Drive and walk north to Northmount Drive.
7. Turn left and walk west on Northmount Drive.
8. Turn left along the east side of Brentwood School and then right around the south side of the school to visit the garden area.
9. Walk north in an alley from the west side of the garden to Northmount Drive.
10. Turn left and walk west to Brisebois Drive.
11. Continue walking west on Northmount Drive.
12. Turn right at the access road to Nose Hill Library.
13. From the library cross to the south side of Northmount Drive, turn right and then turn left on Boulton Road.
14. Follow Boulton Road as it goes south and then east to Bulyea Road.
15. Turn right on Bulyea Road and then left on Brentwood Green.
16. Follow Brentwood Green east past a traffic barrier wall to reach Brisebois Drive.
17. Cross Brisebois Drive and continue east on Brentwood Road back to the station.

Chapter Seven
Dalhousie Station

Station Information: Dalhousie Station is in the centre median of Crowchild Trail just east of 53rd Street NW. The station opened in 2003. Stairs, escalators and an elevator at the east end of the centre platform provide access to the pedestrian overpasses for the north and south sides of Crowchild Trail. The far end of both overpasses is at ground level. A park and ride lot and numerous bus stops are on the north side of Crowchild Trail. The station has a heated waiting area.

The development of the community of Varsity Acres on the south side of Crowchild Trail began in the early 1960s. The area on the north side of the station that is now Dalhousie was annexed by the city in 1961 with development of the community starting in 1967. Dalhousie Station shopping centre is west of the station park and ride lot. The shopping centre and station parking lot are on the site of a former trailer court that relocated to an area just west of Crowfoot Station.

Dalhousie Walk 1
Edgemont Ravines to Dalhousie Station

Walk Overview: This linear route starts in the northeast corner of Edgemont following a path through two ravines. These ravines encompass an area of about 35.5 hectares. After leaving the ravines the route continues downhill to the south side of the community beside John Laurie Boulevard. The route then crosses a pedestrian overpass into Dalhousie and follows a path through a green space back to the station.

Length: 6.4 km

Route Description & Accessibility: Most of the route is on paved paths or sidewalks. One short section in Edgemont on a gravel access road has poor accessibility. An alternate route for this section is included in the text. The first part of the route in the first ravine has a long gradual ascent. When that ascent ends most of the remainder of the route to the station is a long gradual descent.

Food and Drink: Along the route you pass a convenience store. In the Dalhousie Station shopping centre adjacent to the station there are several restaurants, a coffee shop, a grocery store and a gas station convenience store.

Washrooms: There are no public washrooms along this route.

Map References: Clear-View – 4 & 9, MapArt – 143
Rand McNally – 14, 13 & 25, Sherlock – 10, 9 & 17

Route Category: Bus/Walk – Ride the bus to the start of the route and walk back to the station.

Bus Directions from the station to the start of the walk: Turn left at the upper level of the station to reach the bus area on the north side of Crowchild Trail. Catch bus # 54 Edgevalley at stop 4022. Get off at stop 8010 on westbound Edgebrook Boulevard at Edgeridge View. This stop is 15 minutes from the station. The bus frequency is 30 minutes during mid-day on weekdays or Saturdays and 45 minutes on Sundays. For Dalhousie Walk 7 Hidden Valley the route starts at the same bus stop.

The Walk: Edgemont is the largest residential community in Calgary. Development of Edgemont started in the late 1970s. The upper portion of the community is at about the same altitude as the plateau area of Nose Hill Park. From this Edgemont Plateau escarpment slopes lead down to the lower sections of the community. There are also several ravines in the community.

Edgemont Ravines Wetlands just west of Edgebrook Boulevard

Walk a few steps back from the bus stop and use the crosswalk to reach the west side of Edgebrook Boulevard. A paved path leads west into the Edgemont Ravines Park. The route soon passes a wetlands area on your left. This is an excellent location to view waterfowl. Soon after the wetlands the path begins a gradual ascent up through the ravine. Near the top of the ascent you reach a junction (1.4 km). The right branch leads up to a path beside Country Hills Boulevard. Your route follows the left branch and climbs a few steps more before leveling off. The path turns to the left and begins the long descent heading southwesterly through the second ravine. At this point you begin to get some views towards the south. Ignore any paths leading off left or right from the main path.

After the path makes a major bend to the left and heads southeasterly you pass an area with three small rabbit sculptures. A playground on the left is just beyond the sculptures (2.6 km). The main path then bends to the right and goes up a little rise past some tennis courts to where the path turns left along the north side of Edgepark Boulevard. At the three way stop for Edgepark Boulevard and Edgemont Boulevard cross to the east side of Edgemont Boulevard. Turn right to continue the long descent in a southwesterly direction (3.0 km).

Path in Edgemont Ravines

The route passes the World Health Club building. At Edgemont Drive turn left after crossing to the south side of the road (4.1 km). Turn right when you reach the gravel access road for an athletic park. Follow the road to the parking lot. If a better walking surface than the gravel road is required, continue to walk east on the south side of Edgemont Drive to where you join a path across from Edgemont Hill. From the parking area for the athletic park follow the paved path between some tennis courts and basketball courts on the right and a fenced city utility area on the left. The path turns left along the top edge of a slope leading down to some playing fields and an outdoor skating rink. Stay on the path as it curves to the right and heads south along the west side of Edgemont Drive. The detour route joins this path. The path leads to a pedestrian overpass above John Laurie Boulevard (4.8 km).

Cross the overpass into Dalhousie. The route continues downhill although the descent is now more gradual than the earlier part of the walk. Cross Dalsby Gate and continue between houses that back onto the green space. Walk past St. Dominic's School and cross Dalhart Road at the crosswalk (5.4 km). The school's namesake, Dominic Savio, was born in Italy in 1842, spending much of his short life of 15 years devoted to prayer and caring for others.

The route continues on a gradual descent in another green space behind houses until you reach Dalhousie Drive (5.8 km). Turn left and walk a few steps to the pedestrian crossing light to reach the south side of Dalhousie Drive. Turn right and after a few steps west, turn left and follow the path south past some tennis courts. The parking lot and bus stop area for Dalhousie Station are now on the right. Take a path to the right through a gateway in a wire fence and turn left. Follow the sidewalk south past the bus stop area to the station overpass (6.4 km).

Route Summary:
1. Cross the pedestrian overpass to the bus stop area on the north side of Crowchild Trail.
2. Catch bus # 54 Edgevalley at stop 4022. Get off at stop 8010 on westbound Edgebrook Boulevard at Edgeridge View.
3. Use the crosswalk to reach the west side of Edgebrook Boulevard.
4. Follow the paved path leading west in Edgemont Ravines Park past a wetlands area on the left.
5. The path gradually ascends to a junction.
6. Take the left branch as it climbs a few steps more before leveling off.
7. The path turns left and begins a long descent through a second ravine. Ignore any paths leading left or right off the main path.
8. The path makes a major bend to the left and passes a playground.
9. The path bends to the right and goes up a little rise past some tennis courts and then turns left along the north side of Edgepark Boulevard.

10. At the intersection of Edgepark Boulevard with Edgemont Boulevard cross to the east side of the road and turn right continuing the long descent.
11. At Edgemont Drive cross to the south side of the road and turn left.
12. Turn right and follow a gravel access road for an athletic park.
13. From the parking lot follow the path between tennis courts and a fenced city utility area.
14. The path turns left and then makes a curve to the right along the west side of Edgemont Drive to the pedestrian overpass above John Laurie Boulevard.
15. Cross the pedestrian overpass into Dalhousie.
16. Follow the path south and cross Dalsby Gate.
17. The path leads past St. Dominic School and crosses Dalhart Road.
18. Continue south on the path to the north side of Dalhousie Drive.
19. Turn left and walk a few steps to the pedestrian crossing light to reach the south side of Dalhousie Drive.
20. Turn right and after a few steps turn left walking south past tennis courts.
21. Take a path to the right through a gateway in a wire fence.
22. Turn left walking past the bus stop area to the pedestrian overpass.

Dalhousie Walk 2
Edgemont, Hawkwood & Ranchlands

Walk Overview: This linear route travels through short sections of green space in three adjacent communities. There are several excellent viewpoints along the route.

Length: 3.2 km

Route Description & Accessibility: Accessibility on this route is poor. There are a lot of ascents/descents on the route. Some of the walking surface is dirt trails with other sections of the route on sidewalks or paved paths. No alternate route is listed in the text.

Food and Drink: Along the route you pass a gas station convenience store in Ranchlands. In Dalhousie Station shopping centre adjacent to the station there are several restaurants, a coffee shop, a grocery store and a gas station convenience store.

Washrooms: There are no public washrooms along the route.

Map References: Clear-View – 3, MapArt – 143
Rand McNally – 25, Sherlock – 9

Route Category: Bus/Walk/Bus – Ride the bus to the start of the route and when finished the walk ride the bus back to the station.

Bus Directions from the station to the start of the route: Turn left at the upper level of the station building and cross the overpass above Crowchild Trail to the bus stop area. Catch bus # 154 Hamptons at stop 4022. Get off at stop 4015 on northbound Edgedale Drive at Edgehill Drive. This stop is 8 minutes from the station. The bus frequency is 30 minutes during mid-day on weekdays or Saturdays and 45 minutes on Sundays.

The Walk: After getting off the bus cross to the west side of Edgedale Drive. Ahead of you is a shallow ravine with trees. Look for a dirt trail and start to follow it on a gradual ascent through the treed area. There is a second alternate trail to the right that crosses the south-facing slope around the edge of the treed area. At the top end of the ravine, look for a set of stairs leading up to a path overlooking Sarcee Trail.

Follow the path across the pedestrian overpass (0.4 km) that connects Edgemont with the community of Hawkwood on the west side of Sarcee Trail. Hawkwood is named for John and Joseph Hawkwood who farmed in this area. The land was annexed in 1961 but the development did not start until 1981. The north end of the community is at about the same altitude as the upper part of Edgemont.

On the west side of the overpass climb a short set of stairs to a three-way junction. A paved path is on the left. On the right a longer set of stairs leads down into a ravine. Your route follows a trail straight ahead up a small ascent heading in a northwesterly direction. On the left down the slope are the houses on Hawkcliff Way. To the right is a treed slope leading down into the ravine. Along this section of trail there are excellent views to the south and west.

As the trail nears Hawkcliff Way descend a short steep slope to the corner where Hawkcliff Way meets Hawkcliff Gate (0.8 km). Follow Hawkcliff Gate one short block west to Hawkwood Boulevard. Turn left and walk downhill to the traffic lights at Hawkwood Boulevard and John Laurie Boulevard. On the way down the hill you pass St. Thomas United Church, named for one of the twelve apostles of Jesus.

Cross to the south side of John Laurie Boulevard and climb a short set of stairs (1.4 km) going through a gateway in the fence into Ranchland Estates Drive Green Space, also known as Ranchlands Park. This 12 hectares green space is very popular with dog walkers. The area now occupied by Ranchlands was annexed in 1961 with the development of the community starting in 1977.

As you enter Ranchland Estates Drive Green Space turn left and follow a trail that parallels the fence. At the first junction turn right and follow

View looking southwest from the west side
of the Hawkwood-Edgemont pedestrian overpass

the trail uphill to where there are more excellent views. Continue along the
trail keeping to the right at the next two junctions. The trail leads to Ranch
Estates Drive (1.9 km).

Go through the gateway in the fence, cross to the south side of Ranch
Estates Drive and pass through a gateway in another fence to enter another
natural area. Follow a trail keeping a treed area on your right. The trail then
turns to the left and crosses a small open space to a second treed area.
Look for a trail on the right that enters the trees. Watch carefully as this trail
can be easy to miss. This short trail is very pleasant although it can be
muddy at times.

If you do miss the turn into the trees the trail to the left reaches an open
space behind some houses. From here follow a trail that stays close to the
treed area on the right. This trail leads to the same location as the earlier
trail through the trees. Both trails join a paved path where a right turn leads
to Ranch Estates Drive (2.2 km). Turn left and walk a few steps south on
Ranch Estates Drive to Ranchview Drive.

Turn right and walk west on Ranchview Drive to the traffic lights at
Ranchlands Boulevard. Cross to the southwest corner of the intersection and

Trail in Ranchlands Park

walk west on Ranchview Drive turning left onto the grass between the community hall parking lot and the outdoor skating rink boards. On the left is Thunder Hill (so named by students at Ranchlands School). To the right is St. Rita School named for St. Rita of Cascia, who was born in Italy in 1380. After her husband and children died St. Rita entered an Augustinian convent.

Ascend the hill to where you are overlooking Ranchlands School. This location is an excellent viewpoint. Walk along the crest of the hill and then look for a trail descending the slope on the left towards some tennis courts (2.8 km). On the south side of the tennis courts a paved path leads across the field to a gateway in the fence on Ranchlands Boulevard. Turn right and walk to the corner where Ranchview Drive joins Ranchlands Boulevard. Cross to the south side of the road and the end of the route.

Bus Directions from the end of the route to the station:
Catch bus # 43 Northwest Loop at stop 7183 on southbound Ranchview Drive a few steps south of Ranchlands Boulevard (3.2 km). Get off the bus at stop 4002 back at the station. The scheduled time back to the station is 8 minutes. The bus frequency is 30 minutes during mid-day on weekdays and 45 minutes on Saturdays or Sundays.

Route Summary:

1. From the upper level of the station use the pedestrian overpass to access the bus stop area on the north side of Crowchild Trail.
2. Catch bus # 154 Hamptons at stop 4022. Get off at stop 4015 on northbound Edgedale Drive at Edgehill Drive.
3. From the bus stop cross to the west side of Edgedale Drive.
4. Follow a trail ascending through a treed area in a shallow ravine.
5. Near the top end of the ravine climb a set of stairs up to a path overlooking Sarcee Trail.
6. Follow the path across a pedestrian overpass into the community of Hawkwood.
7. Climb a short set of stairs to a three-way junction on the west side of the overpass. Follow a trail straight ahead from the junction. The left branch from the junction is a path and the right branch is a set of stairs down into a ravine.
8. As the trail nears Hawkcliff Way descend a short steep slope to the intersection of Hawkcliff Way and Hawkcliff Gate.
9. Follow Hawkcliff Gate one short block west to Hawkwood Bouevard.
10. Turn left and walk south on Hawkwood Boulevard as the road descends to the traffic lights at John Laurie Boulevard.
11. Cross to the south side of John Laurie Boulevard and climb a short set of stairs to reach a gateway in the fence on the north side of Ranch Estates Drive Green Space (Ranchlands Park).
12. Turn left following a trail that parallels the fence.
13. At the first junction turn right and follow the trail uphill.
14. Keep to the right at the next two junctions. The trail leads to Ranch Estates Drive.
15. Go through a gateway in the fence, cross Ranch Estates Drive and go through a second gateway into another natural area.
16. Follow a trail keeping a treed area on your right. The trail then turns left crossing a small open space to reach a second treed area.
17. Look for a trail on the right that enters the treed area.
18. The trail leads to a path where you turn right to reach Ranch Estates Drive.
19. Turn left and walk a few steps south to reach Ranchview Drive.
20. Turn right and follow Ranchview Drive west to Ranchlands Boulevard.
21. Cross to the southwest corner of the intersection and walk west on Ranchview Drive turning left onto the grass between the community hall parking lot and the outdoor skating rink boards.
22. Look for a trail that leads to the top of a small hill.
23. Follow the crest of the hill and turn left on a trail descending towards tennis courts.
24. On the south side of the tennis courts a path leads to a gateway in the fence beside Ranchlands Boulevard.

25. Turn right and walk to the corner where Ranchview Drive joins Ranchlands Boulevard. Cross to the south side of the road.
26. Catch bus # 43 Northwest Loop at stop 7183 on southbound Ranchview Drive a few steps south of Ranchlands Boulevard. Get off at stop 4002 at the station.

Dalhousie Walk 3
Edgemont Escarpment

Walk Overview: This linear route follows the top edge of the Edgemont escarpment. There are excellent views throughout the route.

Length: 3.7 km

Route Description & Accessibility: The dirt trails with some ascents/descents make the accessibility of this route very poor. No alternate route is included in the text.

Food and Drink: Stop and sit on some large rocks along the route and enjoy the view. There are no stores or restaurants along this route. In Dalhousie Station shopping centre adjacent to the station there are several restaurants, a coffee shop, a grocery store and a gas station convenience store.

Washrooms: There are no public washrooms along the route.

Map References: Clear-View – 4, MapArt - 143
Rand McNally – 26 & 25, Sherlock – 9

Route Category: Bus/Walk/Bus – Ride the bus to the start of the route and when finished the walk ride the bus back to the station.

Bus Directions from the station to the start of the walk:
Catch bus # 77 Edgemont at stop 4023. Get off at stop 7077 on eastbound Edenwold Drive at Edelweiss Drive. This stop is 13 or 14 minutes from the station. The bus frequency is 30 minutes during mid-day on weekdays or Saturdays and 45 minutes on Sundays.

The Walk: After getting off the bus walk east (the same direction as the bus route) on Edenwold Drive and turn right onto Edelweiss Drive. Make a left turn at the next corner onto Edelweiss Crescent. After the road makes a right turn look for a green space on your left (0.3 km). Follow a dirt trail through the green space. Excellent views to the south and east begin to appear along this trail. On the right are the houses on Edelweiss Crescent. On the left the slope leads down to Shaganappi Trail. Beyond Shaganappi Trail is Nose Hill Park. The trail turns to the right and within a short distance

View looking east from Edgemont Escarpment

turns left behind the houses on Edelweiss Drive.

At a junction where a trail leads to the right between houses to Edelweiss Drive the route continues south on the left trail behind the houses that are now on Edelweiss Point. When the route reaches the last of the houses on the east side of Edelweiss Point (1.0 km), turn to the right around the last houses and begin walking north behind the houses on the west side of Edelweiss Point. After making this turn there is a panoramic view west towards the mountains.

Continue walking north past the houses on the right with the downhill slope on the left. Just before reaching Edenwold Drive make another major turn (1.9 km) following a trail to the left down a small slope and then up another slope to where the route is now behind the houses on Edenstone Road. The route is heading in a southwesterly direction. The trail then turns to the left heading south behind the houses on Edenstone Way.

At the point where there is a major turn to the right you reach some large sandstone rocks (2.4 km). The trail soon makes another right turn and starts to head in a northerly direction. At the bottom of the slope is Edgemont

Looking southwest from the Edgemont Escarpment

Boulevard. Stop for a moment and see if you can pick out some of the viewpoint locations on Dalhousie Walk 2 – Edgemont, Hawkwood and Ranchlands. As you continue north there are some sections of the route where the view is blocked by trees on the left. The length of the slope is decreasing as Edgemont Boulevard continues to climb uphill. There is another right turn near the end of the route and the intersection where Edenwold Drive and Edgevalley Drive meet Edgemont Boulevard. Cross to the north side of Edgemont Boulevard to the end of the route.

Bus Directions from the end of the route to the station:
Catch bus # 77 Edgemont at stop 6399 on westbound Edgemont Boulevard at Edgevalley Drive (3.7 km). Get off at stop 4023 at the station. The scheduled time back to the station is 12 minutes. The bus frequency is 30 minutes during mid-day on weekends or Saturdays and 45 minutes on Sundays.

Route Summary:
1. Catch bus # 77 Edgemont at stop 4023. Get off at stop 7077 on eastbound Edenwold Drive and Edelweiss Road.
2. After getting off the bus walk east (the same direction as the bus route) on Edenwold Drive and turn right onto Edelweiss Drive.

3. Make a left turn at the next corner onto Edelweiss Crescent.
4. After the road makes a right turn look for a green space on the left.
5. Follow a dirt trail through the green space.
6. The trail turns right and within a short distance turns left.
7. Keep left at a junction where a trail leads to the right between houses.
8. When the route reaches the last of the houses on the right make a turn to the right and begin walking north.
9. Continue walking north and just before Edenwold Drive take a trail on the left down a small slope and then up another slope to where you are now behind the houses on Edenstone Road.
9. The trail then turns left.
10. There is a major turn to the right by the large sandstone rocks.
11. The route soon makes another right turn and heads north.
12. Near the end of the route there is another right turn before you reach the intersection where Edenwold Drive & Edgevalley Drive meet Edgemont Boulevard.
13. Cross to the northwest corner of this intersection. Catch bus # 77 Edgemont at stop 6399 on westbound Edgemont Boulevard at Edgevalley Drive. Get off at stop 4023 at the station.

Dalhousie Walk 4
Bowmont Park (Waterfall Valley)

Walk Overview: Most of this route is a large loop with a short out-and-back section near the start/finish and a second out-and-back section near the middle of the loop. The route passes through Varsity Estates and goes down into the aptly named Waterfall Valley ravine in Bowmont Park. The park is a 164 hectares natural area with a mix of forest, grasslands and escarpment slopes leading up to a plateau. Some sections of the route are isolated so use your own discretion about walking alone.

Length: 9.1 km

Route Description & Accessibility: Large sections of the route in Bowmont Park have poor accessibility. There are two long descents and two equally long ascents. There are also some smaller ascents/descents. The walking surface is a mix of sidewalks, paved paths and dirt trails. No alternate routes are included in the text.

Food and Drink: There are benches beside the path in Bowmont Park. The route passes Silver Springs Plaza after about 3 km. There is a restaurant, a coffee shop and a bakery in Crowchild Square shopping centre adjacent to the station.

Washrooms: There are no public washrooms along this route.
Map References: Clear-View – 9, 8 & 16, MapArt – 143 & 153
Rand McNally – 24 & 36, Sherlock – 17 & 16
Route Category: Walk - The route starts and ends at the station (no bus is required).
The Walk: At the upper level of the station building turn right and cross the pedestrian overpass to the south side of Crowchild Trail. Follow the path to the right past the back of Bow Valley Church parking lot and Crowchild Square shopping centre. At the time of writing there are detour signs to follow as this section of path is closed due to the construction of a large condo building on the east side of the shopping centre. The path turns left on the west side of the shopping centre and ends at a t-intersection at 53rd Street and Varsity Estates Drive (0.6 km). Cross to the west side of 53rd Street and start heading west along Varsity Estates Drive.

Along this section of road there are glimpses from time to time of Silver Springs Golf & Country Club. The road then makes a major turn to the left and starts heading south. At 700 Varsity Estates Place make a right turn and walk by the houses on this cul-de-sac (2.1 km). At the end of the road follow a paved path past a former bus trap to Silver Springs Gate in the community of Silver Springs. This community, established in 1972, is named for the underground springs that flow into the Bow River.

Turn left and follow the path west on the south side of Silver Springs Gate past some playing fields and the Springfield Condos to the traffic light at Silver Springs Boulevard (2.9 km). Silver Springs Plaza shopping centre is on the north side of Silver Springs Gate at this corner.

Turn left at the light and walk south to the end of Silver Springs Boulevard where park users can park on the west side of the road or at the south end of the road. At this point look for the path leading into Bowmont Park. On the right is the top end of Waterfall Valley ravine. The path soon splits. Follow the right branch down into the ravine. The route returns to this junction and follows the left branch after visiting Waterfall Valley.

At the point where the path levels off in the ravine, there are interpretive signs on the left. This is the start of Waterfall Valley trail (3.4 km). The trail descends into the ravine along a dirt trail and wooden walkways. There are several information plaques along the route. At the bottom end of the trail you reach a viewpoint (3.9 km) overlooking the Bow River and the community of Bowness across the river. Look for the waterfalls trickling down the slopes towards the river. This is a good spot to stop and relax and/or take pictures.

When you are ready begin your ascent back through the ravine and turn

Steps leading down into Waterfall Valley

right when you reach the paved path. At the first junction after climbing out of the ravine take the right branch. The path stays close to Silverview Drive for only a short time before beginning a long descent to the floodplain area of Bowmont Park. There is a viewpoint location along this section of the path. There is a large island in the river.

At the bottom of the slope look for the dirt trail leading to the left into a treed area (5.7 km). Before following this trail you might want to spend a few minutes to the right of the path on the nearby bank of the river. The trail leads east along the bottom edge of the escarpment slope to an open space at the south end of another ravine. This ravine is part of the Silver Springs Golf and Country Club property. Dalhousie Walk 5 – Bowmont Park East also passes through this area. The escarpment slope you were walking beside turns north and becomes the west slope of the ravine. The route climbs the slope on the east side of the ravine. When the trail splits partway up the slope take the left branch. The right branch is on Dalhousie Walk 5 – Bowmont Park East.

At the top of the slope you are at the west end of 40th Avenue in Varsity Acres. Turn left onto Varsity Road (6.6 km) and then turn left onto Varsity

Steps near the bottom of Waterfall Valley

Drive and follow this road to 53ʳᵈ Street (7.2 km). East of 53ʳᵈ Street on Varsity Drive is F.E. Osborne School. Osborne came to Calgary in 1905 and established Osborne's Books specializing in stationery and school supplies. The store was destroyed by fire in 1966. Osborne served as a city alderman for two terms and was mayor from 1927 to 1929. East of Osborne School is Marion Carson School. Marion Carson came to Calgary in 1893 and helped establish the first TB sanatorium in Alberta. She also served as a school trustee and was a member of the library board. In 1946 she was recognized as Calgary's citizen of the year.

From the corner by Osborne School turn left and head north on 53ʳᵈ Street down a short descent. This short section of route from Varsity Drive to the bottom of the short descent is also on Dalhousie Walk 5. Near the end of the descent you pass the Margaret Brown Memorial Garden on the east side of 53ʳᵈ Street. The garden is lovingly cared for in the summer by a group of dedicated volunteers. Nearby is one of five pedestal-shaped public art displays located in Varsity Acres. Each of the pedestals features a display of youth art. This route passes a second pedestal near the end of this walk. The memorial garden and this pedestal are also on the route for Walk 5. The

One of the pedestal shaped art displays on 53rd Street

third of the five pedestals is also on Walk 5. The other two pedestals are located on Varsity Drive at Shaganappi Trail and at 37th Street.

The route continues north up a short ascent on 53rd Street to the t-intersection at 53rd Street and Varsity Estates Drive. Make a left turn and after a short descent make a right turn onto Varsity Estates Rise (7.7 km). On Varsity Estates Rise the route reaches a large community park on the right. Angle across the grass and exit the park where Varsity Estates Road meets 53rd Street across from Crowchild Square shopping centre. There is a small rest area with a bench and a second art pedestal near the northeast corner of the park.

Use the pedestrian crossing light to cross to the shopping centre side of the road and turn left. At the nearby t-intersection retrace your steps back along the path behind the shopping centre and the church to the station (9.1 km).

Route Summary:
1. From the upper level of the station turn right and cross the pedestrian overpass to the south side of Crowchild Trail.
2. Follow the path to the right as it passes by the back of Bow Valley Church parking lot and Crowchild Square shopping centre.
3. The path turns left on the west side of the shopping centre and ends at a t-intersection on 53rd Street and Varsity Estates Drive.
4. Cross to the west side of 53rd Street and walk west along Varsity Estates Drive.
5. The road makes a major turn to the left and starts heading south.
6. Turn right at 700 Varsity Estates Place.

7. At the end of the road follow a path that leads to Silver Springs Gate.
8. Turn left and follow the path on the south side of Silver Springs Gate past some playing fields and the Springfield Condos to the traffic light at Silver Springs Boulevard.
9. Turn left and walk south to the end of Silver Springs Boulevard.
10. Follow a path leading into Bowmont Park.
11. At a junction take the right branch.
12. Follow the path down into Waterfall Valley.
13. Just before the path begins to ascend turn left onto a dirt trail leading down into Waterfall Valley.
14. Follow the trail and some wooden walkways down to a viewpoint overlooking the Bow River.
15. Retrace your steps back up Waterfall Valley and turn right on the path climbing up the side of the ravine to the first junction.
16. Take the right branch following the path as it begins a long descent to the floodplain area of Bowmont Park.
17. At the bottom of the slope turn left and follow a trail leading along the base of the escarpment slope.
18. When you reach an open space south of the ravine follow a trail ascending the slope on the east side of a ravine.
19. When the trail splits partway up the hill take the left branch.
20. When the trail reaches the west end of 40th Avenue turn left onto Varsity Road, then left on Varsity Drive to reach 53rd Street.
21. Turn left and follow 53rd Street down a short descent and up a short ascent to a t-intersection with Varsity Estates Drive.
22. Turn left on Varsity Estates Drive going down a short descent and make a right turn onto Varsity Estates Rise.
23. Follow this road north and angle to the right across a large park to reach the corner of Varsity Estates Drive and 53rd Street across from Crowchild Square shopping centre.
24. Cross to the north side of the road and retrace your earlier route back to the station.

Dalhousie Walk 5
Bowmont Park East

Walk Overview: This route has two out-and-back sections connected to a loop. The walk passes through a shallow ravine on the way to the eastern part of Bowmont Park. Some sections of the route are isolated so use your own discretion about walking alone.

The site of Bowmont Park was once part of the Cochrane Ranche property. The Cochrane Ranche Company was the first of many large ranches in Western Canada. The company leased over 100,000 acres. In 1881, the company purchased their first cattle. Senator Matthew H. Cochrane of Quebec was the president of the company.

Length: 8.8 km

Route Description & Accessibility: The walking surface for most of the route is paved paths. The paved path in the shallow ravine has small ascents/descents. However accessibility on the escarpment slope in Bowmont Park is poor. No alternate routes are included in the text.

Food and Drink: There are benches along the path in Bowmont Park. There is a restaurant, a coffee shop and a bakery in Crowchild Square shopping centre adjacent to the station.

Washrooms: There are no public washrooms on this route.

Map References: Clear-View – 9 & 16, MapArt – 143 & 153
Rand McNally – 24 & 36, Sherlock – 17

Route Category: Walk - The route starts and ends at the station (no bus is required).

The Walk: At the upper level of the station building turn right and cross the overpass to the south side of Crowchild Trail. Make a left turn on a path that leads towards another path and a second pedestrian overpass above Crowchild Trail.

Follow this path to the right walking south through a shallow ravine with houses backing onto both sides of the green area. The path makes a turn to the right going west up a short ascent to reach 53rd Street (1.2 km). On the left just before 53rd Street is the Margaret Brown Memorial Garden with a dedication plaque. This rest stop is lovingly cared for in the summer by a group of dedicated volunteers. Nearby is one of five pedestal-shaped public art displays in Varsity Acres. Each pedestal features a display of youth art. You pass a second of these pedestals in a small park to your right just before you reach 40th Avenue. A third pedestal is on the route for Walk 4. The other two pedestals are located on Varsity Drive at Shaganappi Trail and at 37th Street.

Shouldice Bridge, ca. 1931. Glenbow Archives NA-1887-1

Turn left on 53rd Street up a small ascent to Varsity Drive. Continue south on 53rd Street to where it ends at 40th Avenue (2.0 km). Use the pedestrian crossing light to reach the northeast corner of Bowmont Park. At this point a panoramic view opens up to the southwest. Walk south on the paved path past the houses on the left. After passing a small playground the path is closer to the top edge of the escarpment. At 32nd Avenue turn right and cross over an access road leading down to the floodplain where a former gravel pit business was located. The above photo of Shouldice Bridge in 1931 was probably taken from a spot close to where the access road starts down the slope. The city is planning to reclaim the former gravel pit site thus increasing the size of Bowmont Park. At the time of writing the area is fenced off to the general public.

From the top of the escarpment on the west side of the access road a dirt trail descends south down the slope to a parking lot for Bowmont Park (2.8 km). Bowmont Park encompasses the escarpment slope west from this point to Nose Hill Drive plus the plateau area at the top of the escarpment and the floodplain area between the base of the escarpment and the river. The park is 164 hectares in size. The park name derives from combining the first syllables of Bowness and Montgomery communities.

From the parking lot follow the path through a gateway in the park fence. There is another of the Bowmont Park viewpoints by the gateway. From the

Riverbank erosion in Bowmont Park

viewpoint the path heads north gradually descending to the floodplain. At the end of the descent the path turns left and heads northwesterly on the floodplain. There is a rough trail closer to the river if you want to explore. The path reaches an open area on your right on the west side of the gravel pit fence (4.5 km). The route returns to this open area after exploring the area to the west. Continue walking on the path until you reach the base of the escarpment where the path makes a long ascent up the steep slope. The base of the escarpment is the turn around point for this route. Dalhousie Walk 4 comes down this steep path and turns left to follow a trail east through a treed area at the base of the escarpment.

Retrace your steps a short distance and turn right onto a trail that leads through the wooded area. At one point the trail is by the edge of the river. When the trail ends back at the path turn right and retrace your earlier route back to the open area.

Turn left and follow the trail north through the open area towards the bottom end of a ravine. The ravine area north of a fence line is the Silver Springs Golf Course property. When you reach the point where the escarpment slopes on both sides of the ravine starts, turn right and follow a trail that ascends the slope. At a junction take the right branch that stays closer to the top edge of the escarpment. Near the top of the slope take the right branch at a junction. The short section of trail from the bottom of the slope to the junction is also on Dalhousie Walk 4.

Follow the trail east along the top of the escarpment to the turnaround loop for bus # 9 Varsity Acres (6.5 km). Cross to the north side of 40th Avenue, turn right and walk east on the sidewalk to 53rd Street (7.3 km). Turn left and head north on 53rd Street retracing your earlier route to the ravine north of Varsity Drive. Follow the ravine back to the station (8.8 km).

Route Summary:

1. From the upper level of the station turn right and cross the pedestrian overpass to the south side of Crowchild Trail.
2. Turn left to reach a path that crosses a second pedestrian overpass.
3. Take the path to the right and head south through a shallow ravine.
4. When the path reaches 53rd Street turn left and follow the road south to where 53rd Street ends at 40th Avenue.
5. Cross to the southwest corner and follow a path leading south through Bowmont Park.
6. When the path ends at 32nd Avenue turn right crossing an access road and follow a dirt trail down the slope to a parking lot for Bowmont Park.
7. Follow a path to the right through a gateway in a fence.
8. This path heads north on a gradual descent to the floodplain.
9. The path heads northwest to where a trail leads north towards the bottom end of a ravine. The route follows this trail later.
10. Keep walking on the path until it reaches the bottom of the escarpment.
11. Retrace your route a few steps and turn right onto a trail leading through a treed area.
12. Follow the trail and when it joins the path turn right and retrace your steps back to the open area.
13. Turn left and follow the trail north through the open area to the bottom end of a ravine.
14. Ascend a trail on the slope to your right. At a junction follow the right branch that stays closer to the top edge of the escarpment.
15. Follow the trail east along the top of the escarpment until you reach the turn around loop for bus # 9 Varsity Acres.
16. Cross to the north side of 40th Avenue turn right and follow the sidewalk to 53rd Street.
17. Turn left and retrace your earlier route north on 53rd Street and through the ravine back to the station.

Dalhousie Walk 6
Nose Hill Park (Meadowlark Prairie)

Walk Overview: This route has an out-and-back section joined to a loop. Most of the route is on the Nose Hill Park plateau on the east side of Shaganappi Trail. The views to the west are excellent. Depending on the time of day you choose for your walk you may not meet many other walkers on this route so use discretion if you are concerned about walking alone on what might be an isolated route.

Length: 6.0 km

Route Description & Accessibility: The walking surface is a mix of sidewalks, paths and trails. There are some ascents/descents but no long steep sections. The path in the first half of the route is relatively flat. When you reach the very uneven dirt trail near the halfway point, accessibility on that trail becomes very difficult. It is suggested you retrace the first part of the route back along the path.

Food and Drink: There is a gas station convenience store near the start/finish of this route.

Washrooms: There is a public washroom building in Nose Hill Park at the intersection of Shaganappi Trail and Edgemont Boulevard.

Map References: Clear-View – 4, MapArt – 143 & 144 Rand McNally – 26, Sherlock – 9 & 10

Route Category: Bus/Walk/Bus – Ride the bus to the start of the route and when finished the walk, ride the bus back to the station.

Bus Directions from the station to the start of the walk: Cross the pedestrian overpass to the north side of Crowchild Trail. Catch bus # 77 Edgemont at stop 4023. Get off at stop 7080 on northbound Edgebrook Drive just north of Edgemont Boulevard. This stop is 15 minutes from the station. The bus frequency is 30 minutes during mid-day on weekdays or Saturdays and 45 minutes on Sundays.

The Walk: After getting off the bus walk back to the intersection of Edgebrook Drive and Edgemont Boulevard. Turn left and walk east to the traffic lights at Edgemont Boulevard and Shaganappi Trail (0.5 km). Cross to the east side of Shaganappi Trail and turn right walking through the parking lot to where a path leads south into the park. The washroom building is beside the parking lot.

The path from the parking lot is soon joined by a trail on the left that started from the same lot (1.0 km). That trail is on your return route. Keep to the right and continue south on the main path. A path will join from the left

Nose Hill Park – Meadowlark Prairie

(1.6 km). Ignore that path. The path makes a turn to the left and starts going east. The route reaches a junction where the main path turns right and heads south overlooking Many Owls Valley. This junction is where Brentwood Walk 2 turns around (3.0 km). Rough trails lead south and north from the junction.

Make a left turn at the junction and head north on the trail. At a junction with another trail continue straight ahead. At a second junction (4.1 km), a path on the right descends eastbound on the north side of Porcupine Valley. The path goes through a tunnel under 14th Street just south of Berkley Gate. From the junction take the path on the left heading back towards the parking lot. Stay on the main path ignoring any trails leading off left or right. In a treed area on the right there are some picnic tables. The route reaches a four-way junction (5.1 km). The left and centre branches from this junction were on the earlier portion of the route. Take the trail to the right going up a small ascent on the way back to the parking lot.

From the parking lot cross to the west side of Shaganappi Trail and retrace your earlier route back along Edgemont Boulevard to Edgebrook Drive. Cross to the southwest corner of Edgemont Boulevard and Edenwold Drive (6.0 km) where the route ends.

Bus Directions from the end of the route to the station: Catch bus # 77 Edgemont at stop 7083 on southbound Edenwold Drive just south of Edgemont Boulevard. Get off at stop 4023 back at the station. The scheduled time back to the station is 17 minutes. The bus frequency is 30 minutes during mid-day on weekdays or Saturdays and 45 minutes on Sundays.

Route Summary:

1. From the upper level of the station turn left and cross the pedestrian overpass to the north side of Crowchild Trail.
2. Catch bus # 77 Edgemont at stop 4023. Get off at stop 7080 on northbound Edgebrook Drive just north of Edgemont Boulevard.
3. After getting off the bus walk back to the traffic lights at Edgemont Boulevard and Edgebrook Drive.
4. Turn left and walk east to the traffic lights at Edgemont Boulevard and Shaganappi Trail.
5. Cross to the east side of Shaganappi Trail and turn right walking through the parking lot to where a path leads south into the park.
6. The path from the parking lot is soon joined by a trail on the left that also started at the parking lot.
7. Keep to the right and continue south on the main path.
8. A path will join from the left. Ignore that path.
9. The path will make a turn to the left and start heading east.
10. When you reach a junction where the main path turns right, make a left turn and follow a dirt trail north.
11. At a junction with another trail continue straight ahead.
12. At the next junction take the path on the left back to the parking lot.
13. Stay on the main path ignoring any trails leading left or right.
14. At a four-way junction take the trail on the right up a small ascent to the parking lot.
15. From the parking lot cross back to the west side of Shaganappi Trail and retrace your earlier route back to Edgemont Boulevard and Edgemont Drive.
17. Cross to the south side of Edgemont Boulevard.
18. Catch bus # 77 Edgemont at stop 7083 on southbound Edenwold Drive just south of Edgemont Boulevard. Get off at stop 4023 back at the station.

Dalhousie Walk 7
Hidden Valley

Walk Overview: The route starts in the northeast corner of Edgemont at the same bus stop as Dalhousie Walk 1. The walk is a mix of out-and-back and a loop. The walk goes through tunnels under Shaganappi Trail and Country Hills Boulevard before entering the community of Hidden Valley. Between the two tunnels the route crosses through the northwest corner of the community of MacEwan. After making a loop retrace the earlier route back through the tunnels to a bus stop near the start of the walk.

Length: 5.7 km

Route Description & Accessibility: There is one short downhill switchback section of steep pathway near the halfway point of the route. Later there is an uphill section of path. To avoid these two sections you retrace your earlier route back to the second tunnel from the lake. There is a trail along the west side of Hidden Valley Lake. The east side of the lake has poor accessibility as you have to cross the sloped grass beside the lake. For better accessibility retrace your steps along the west side of the lake. Most of the remainder of the route has some small ascents/descents but no big hills.

Food and Drink: There is a convenience store near the halfway point of the walk.

Washrooms: There are no public washrooms along this route.

Map References: Clear-View – 4 & 5, MapArt – 143, 144 & 134
Rand McNally – 14, Sherlock – 10 & 4

Route Category: Bus/Walk/Bus – Ride the bus to the start of the route and when finished the walk, ride the bus back to the station.

Bus Directions from the station to the start of the walk: Turn left at the upper level of the station and cross the overpass to the bus area on the north side of Crowchild Trail. Catch bus # 54 Edgevalley at stop 4022. Get off at stop 8010 on westbound Edgebrook Boulevard at Edgeridge View. This stop is 15 minutes from the station. This bus stop is also the starting point for Walk 1 Edgemont Ravines to Dalhousie Station. The bus frequency is 30 minutes during mid-day on weekends or Saturdays and 45 minutes on Sundays.

The Walk: A paved path on the east side of Edgebrook Boulevard just south of Edgeridge View is the starting point for this route. The path wanders across an open green space and past some playing fields before making a couple of turns down a small descent to the west end of the tunnel under Shaganappi Trail (0.7 km).

One of the pathway tunnels

On the east side of the tunnel the route passes through a treed green space in the northwest corner of MacEwan. MacEwan Ridge Gate (1.0 km) is the only road you cross before reaching the second tunnel. MacEwan Ridge Gate provides access to the Heritage Village housing complex in the northwest corner of MacEwan.

The second tunnel leads under Country Hills Boulevard into Hidden Valley (1.4 km). Development in the community of Hidden Valley started in 1991. On the north side of the tunnel the houses on Hidden Green are on your left and a ravine is on your right. When the path reaches Hidden Valley Drive turn right and head east along the south side of the road. Look for a trail on the right after passing Hidden Circle (2.0 km). The trail leads through a green space between houses to Hidden Valley Lake.

The counterclockwise circuit around is the lake is about 500 metres. Sometimes you may spot birds on this lake. The first part of the circuit along the west side of the lake follows a trail. For the second part of the circuit on the east side of the lake the route is on grass on an angled slope behind the houses on Hidden Valley Heights. Near the northeast corner of the lake turn right and follow a green space between houses to Hidden Valley Heights. Turn left and walk a few steps to reach Hidden Valley Drive.

Turn right and walk a short distance to reach the three-way stop intersection at Hidden Valley Drive and 14th Street. Cross to the north side of Hidden Valley Drive to where you are standing in front of a small strip mall named Hidden Valley Centre. Angle to the right across the parking area and walk around behind the last business in this mall (2.8 km). Follow a paved path that switchbacks down a slope to reach the main path extending through the community in a northwesterly to southeasterly direction. Turn left and follow this path to a junction (3.4 km).

On your right at this junction is St. Elizabeth Seton School named for a New York widow and the founder of the American Daughters of Charity. She died in 1821. By 1830 the Sisters operated schools and orphanages extending from the New York area to as far away as New Orleans and Cincinnati.

Take the left branch at the junction and at the next two junctions again take the left branch. The path leads up the slope to Hidden Valley Drive (4.0 km). From here cross to the south side of Hidden Valley Drive and retrace the route back through the two tunnels and across the open green space to Edgebrook Boulevard and the end of the route (5.7 km).

Bus Directions from the end of the route to the station:
Cross Edgebrook Boulevard and catch bus # 154 Hamptons at stop 8011 on

Hidden Valley Lake

eastbound Edgebrook Boulevard at Edgeridge View. Get off at stop 4022 at the station. The scheduled time back to the station is 18 minutes. The bus frequency is 30 minutes during mid-day on weekdays or Saturdays and 45 minutes on Sundays.

Route Summary:

1. From the upper level of the station turn left and cross the pedestrian overpass to the bus area on the north side of Crowchild Trail.
2. Catch bus # 54 Edgevalley at stop 4022. Get off at stop 8010 on westbound Edgebrook Boulevard at Edgeridge View.
3. A path on the east side of Edgebrook Boulevard is the starting point for the route.
4. The path wanders through an open green space and past playing fields before making a couple of turns down a small descent to reach the west end of a pedestrian tunnel under Shaganappi Trail.
5. On the east side of the tunnel the path passes through a treed area in the northwest corner of MacEwan.
6. Cross MacEwan Ridge Gate before reaching the second tunnel.
7. The second tunnel leads under Country Hills Boulevard into Hidden Valley.
8. When the path reaches Hidden Valley Drive turn right and head east along the south side of this road.
9. Look for a trail on the right after passing Hidden Circle.
10. The trail leads between houses to a pond listed on maps as Hidden Valley Lake.
11. Turn right and follow a trail around the west side of the pond.
12. Continue around the pond walking on the grass after the trail ends at the south end of the pond.
13. Near the northeast corner of the pond turn right through a green space between houses to Hidden Valley Heights.
14. Turn left and walk a few steps to reach Hidden Valley Drive.
15. Turn right and walk a short distance to the three-way stop for Hidden Valley Drive and 14th Street.
16. Cross to the north side of Hidden Valley Drive to the front of a small strip mall.
17. Angle to the right across the parking area and walk around behind the last business in the mall. Follow a path that switchbacks down a slope to join the main path.
18. Turn left following the main path to a junction.
19. Make a left turn at the junction and at the next two junctions again make left turns.
20. The path leads up a slope to Hidden Valley Drive.
21. Cross to the south side of Hidden Valley Drive and retrace the earlier route back through the tunnels and across the open green space back

to Edgebrook Boulevard.

22. Cross to the west side of Edgebrook Boulevard. Catch bus # 154 Hamptons at stop 8011 on eastbound Edgebrook Boulevard at Edgeridge View. Get off at stop 4022 at the station.

Dalhousie Walk 8
Hamptons

Walk Overview: This route passes through a community park and goes down into a shallow ravine on the western edge of the Hamptons community beside the boundary fence for the Country Club of the Hamptons. One section of the walk on the west side of the ravine is on a street considered part of Citadel. This street is separated from the rest of the community by Sarcee Trail. The route is a mix of linear, out-and-back and loop sections.
Length: 2.1 km
Route Description & Accessibility: Most of this route is on paved paths. The descents/ascents on the slopes of the ravine could make the accessibility of this route a bit challenging.
Food and Drink: There are no locations to purchase food and/or drinks along this route.
Washrooms: There are no public washrooms along this route.
Map References: Clear-View – 4 & 3, MapArt – 143
Rand McNally – 12, Sherlock – 9
Route Category: Bus/Walk/Bus – Ride the bus to the start of the route and when finished the walk, ride the bus back to the station.
Bus Directions from the station to the start of the walk: From the upper level of the station turn left and cross the pedestrian overpass to the bus stop area. Catch bus # 154 Hamptons at stop 4022. Get off at stop 4005 on northbound Hamptons Boulevard at Hamptons Green. This stop is 14 minutes from the station. The bus frequency is 30 minutes during mid-day on weekdays or Saturdays and 45 minutes on Sundays.
The Walk: Walk a few steps back from the stop and turn left into a community park area. Follow a path past tennis courts. Keep to the left at a junction as the path bends to the left. The path leads to Hamptons Boulevard (0.4 km).

Cross Hamptons Boulevard and continue straight ahead on a path that passes under an archway with the name Hamptons Green at the top. When the path reaches the fence for the Country Club of the Hamptons it makes a sharp left turn. For a short section of the path you are passing through an area with the golf course fence on the right and a low wooden wall on the left. The bushes on both sides are growing right up to the edge of the path.

The path then descends into a shallow ravine to a junction near the end of the golf course fence (0.9 km). The left branch of the path is on the return route. Turn right and follow the path to a second junction (1.1 km). Again the left branch at the junction is on the return route. The right branch will lead up out of the ravine and between houses to reach Citadel Green. Turn left and walk along Citadel Green. Keep to the left at an intersection. The road to the right leads to Sarcee Trail. The left branch leads past the houses on Citadel Grove. On the left a path between houses leads back down into the ravine to the second junction you passed earlier (1.6 km). Turn right at the junction and again turn right at the next junction. The path ascends the slope to Hamptons Boulevard. Just before reaching Hamptons Boulevard the path goes through a rather interesting area called Hamptons Grove with numerous small trees. The base of each tree has a cement ring around it. The trees are planted in a rather formal pattern. There is a shaded bench in this area if you want a break.

Continue walking past the trees to Hamptons Boulevard. Turn right and walk a few steps to the end of the route (2.1 km).

Bus Directions from the end of the route to the station:
Catch bus # 54 Edgevalley at stop 8371 on eastbound Hamptons Boulevard at Hampshire Grove. Get off at stop 4022 back at the station. The scheduled time back to the station is 15 minutes. The bus frequency is 30 minutes during mid-day on weekdays or Saturdays and 45 minutes on Sundays.

Route Summary:
1. From the upper level of the station cross the pedestrian overpass to the north side of Crowchild Trail. Catch bus # 154 Hamptons at stop 4022.
2. Get off the bus at stop 4005 on northbound Hamptons Boulevard at Hampton Green.
3. Walk a few steps back from the stop and turn left into a community park.
4. Follow a path past tennis courts keeping left at a junction as the path bends to the left.
5. Cross Hamptons Boulevard and continue straight ahead on a path that passes under an archway with the name Hamptons Green at the top.
6. When the path reaches the fence for the Country Club of the Hamptons it makes a sharp left turn.

Small park on Hamptons Grove

7. The path then drops downhill into a shallow ravine.
8. At the next two junctions take the right branch following the path up out of the ravine and between houses to reach Citadel Green.
9. Turn left and walk along Citadel Green keeping left at an intersection as you follow Citadel Grove to a path on the left between houses.
10. The path leads back down into the ravine.
11. At the next two junctions you turn right.
12. The path leads up out of the ravine to Hamptons Boulevard.
13. Turn to the right at Hamptons Boulevard and walk a few steps to the bus stop. Catch bus # 54 Edgevalley at stop 8371 back to the station. Get off at stop 4022 back at the station.

Chapter Eight
Crowfoot Station

Station Information: At the time of writing this station in the median of Crowchild Trail is the last station on the northwest line. The large commercial area of Crowfoot Crossing is on the north side of Crowfoot Station. Pedestrian overpasses lead to ground level on both sides of Crowchild Trail from the upper level of the station building. Crowfoot Parade overpass is located just west of the station. The bus stop area is on the north side of Crowchild Trail. There is very limited parking in this area. The south side has a large parking area for CTrain patrons. Tuscany station in the median between Tuscany on the south side of Crowchild Trail and Rocky Ridge and Royal Oak on the north side of Crowchild Trail is scheduled to open in 2014.

Scenic Acres community on the south side of Crowchild Trail was developed in the 1980s after being annexed by the city in the 1960s. Prior to the annexation Calgary oilman Sam Nickle had owned 800 acres in this area choosing the name Scenic Acres for his property. Arbour Lake on the north side of Crowfoot Trail was developed in the 1990s. The developer named the community after Arbor Lake, near Newport Beach, California.

Crowfoot Walk One
Citadel to Crowfoot Station

Walk Overview: This linear route follows paths and sidewalks through the communities of Citadel and Arbour Lake. Citadel was developed in the early 1990s. In Arbour Lake the route makes a small detour to a dirt trail that climbs up to a gazebo-like structure on top of a small knoll.
Length: 6.4 km
Route Description & Accessibility: Most of the path in Citadel is relatively flat. There is a slight ascent to reach a traffic light crossing on Country Hills Boulevard. On the Arbour Lake side of Country Hills Boulevard there is a short descent as the path enters the community. The walking surface for most of the route is paved paths or sidewalks. Information on a detour that avoids the steep dirt trail to the gazebo is included in the text.
Food and Drink: Along the route there is a convenience store and a specialty food store. There are also restaurants and coffee shops near the

station.

Washrooms: There are no public washrooms along this route.

Map References: Clear-View – 3 & 2, MapArt – 143 & 133
Rand McNally – 12 & 11, Sherlock – 9, 3, 2 & 8

Route Category: Bus/Walk – Ride the bus to the start of the route and walk back to the station.

Bus Directions from the station to the start of the walk: At the upper level of the station turn right and cross the pedestrian overpass above Crowchild Trail to the bus stop area. Catch bus # 199 Citadel at stop 9876. Get off the bus at stop 6961 on northbound Citadel Gate just north of Country Hills Boulevard. This stop is 10 minutes from the station. The bus frequency is 30 minutes daily.

The Walk: After getting off the bus walk forward to the corner of Citadel Drive and Citadel Gate. Cross to the north side of Citadel Drive and follow a path that heads north between houses into Citadel Park. When the path splits take the left branch heading north past the west side of Citadel Park School (0.6 km). The path leads through a narrow green space between the houses on Citadel Crest Green on the left and Citadel Crest Park on the right. This path ends at Citadel Drive (1.1 km). Turn left and follow the sidewalk west to Citadel Meadow Crescent on the right.

Follow Citadel Meadow Crescent north and then west looking for a path on the right that passes between houses. This path turns left behind the houses and heads west through a green space. On the right a small slope leads up to the south side of Stoney Trail. The path begins to turn south as it passes Pointe of View condo complex. On the left there is now more green space with trees between the path and the houses on Citadel Meadow Close. Cross over Citadel Way (2.1 km) and continue south on the path past the east side of St. Brigid School. St. Brigid of Ireland, who lived from 452 to 524, devoted her life to God, founding a religious community in Killdara.

The green space south of the school is wider with playing fields. As the path nears the south side of the community it angles to the right and heads west up a small ascent beside Country Hills Boulevard to a traffic light at Citadel Way (3.0 km). There is a convenience store on this corner.

Cross to the south side of Country Hills Boulevard and follow the path into Arbour Lake as it descends a slope into a wide bowl shaped area. At a trail junction take the right branch and head south. The path leads past playing fields and ends at Arbour Lake Drive (3.6 km). Turn right and follow Arbour Lake Drive west and then south. There is a treed slope on your left. At Arbour Vista Hill turn left and after a few steps look for a trail on the right climbing up the north side of a knoll to where a gazebo-like structure is located (4.2 km).

Arbour Lake viewpoint gazebo

To avoid the poor accessibility on this knoll stay on Arbour Lake Drive. From the top of the knoll you have an excellent view. Descend the south side of the knoll and follow a path to return to Arbour Lake Drive. Turn left and continue south. After crossing Arbour Lake Way walk past the fenced off area for the Arbour Lake Community Association on the left. There is a community hall and a small lake inside the fenced area. During the Christmas season there is an excellent light display around the lake.

At the next corner there is a specialty food store on the right. Arbour Lake Road is to the right and John Laurie Boulevard is to the left (4.8 km). On the far right corner of the intersection is St. Ambrose School. St. Ambrose who lived from 340 (?) to 397 is remembered as the individual who converted St. Augustine. He also challenged Emperor Theodosius and made him do public penance. Theodosius the Great was the last emperor to rule a united Roman Empire.

Cross to the south side of the road and turn left along the south side of John Laurie Boulevard. Watch for a path on the right leading south between the houses on the right and the Crowfoot West office and retail complex on the left. As the route nears the south end of the Crowfoot Square office and retail complex the path turns to the right and ends at Arbour Grove Close across the road from a Pointe of View condo complex. Turn left and walk a few steps to the next intersection. Arbour Lake Road is on the right and Crowfoot Way is on the left (5.8 km). There is a convenience store on this corner.

Turn left and follow Crowfoot Way to the traffic light. On the left is Crowfoot Crescent and on the right is Crowfoot Circle. Turn right onto Crowfoot Circle and follow it past a traffic circle. Walk past the bus stop area and a small parking lot to reach the overpass to the station (6.4 km).

Route Summary:

1. At the upper level of the station turn right and cross the pedestrian overpass to the bus stop area on the north side of Crowchild Trail.
2. Catch bus # 199 Citadel at stop 9876. Get off the bus at stop 6961 on northbound Citadel Gate just north of Country Hills Boulevard.
3. Walk forward to the corner of Citadel Drive and Citadel Gate.
4. Cross to the north side of Citadel Drive and follow a path that heads north between houses into Citadel Park.
5. When the path splits take the left branch heading north past the west side of Citadel Park School.
6. When the path ends at Citadel Drive turn left and follow the sidewalk west to Citadel Meadow Crescent on your right.
7. Follow Citadel Meadow Crescent north and then west looking for a path on the right that passes between houses.
8. The path turns left behind the houses and heads west through a green space.
9. The path turns left as it passes a Pointe of View condo complex.
10. Cross Citadel Way and continue south on the path past the east side of St. Brigid School.
11. The path angles to the right going up a small ascent and paralleling the north side of Country Hills Boulevard to where it meets Citadel Way at a traffic light.
12. Cross to the south side of Country Hills Boulevard and follow the path into Arbour Lake as it descends into a wide bowl shaped area.
13. At a path junction take the right branch as the path heads south past some playing fields and ends at Arbour Lake Drive.
14. Turn right and follow Arbour Lake Drive west and then south.
15. At Arbour Vista Hill take a small detour to the left and follow a trail on the right up the north side of a small knoll to where a gazebo-like structure is located.
16. Descend the south side of the knoll and follow a path to Arbour Lake

Drive.

17. Turn left and continue south on Arbour Lake Drive.
18. At the traffic lights on John Laurie Boulevard cross to the south side of the road and turn left along the path.
19. Turn right on a path heading south between houses on the right and the Crowfoot West office and retail complex on the left.
20. Near the south end of the Crowfoot Square office and retail complex the path turns right and ends at Arbour Grove Close.
21. Turn left and walk a few steps to the traffic light.
22. Cross to the south side of Crowfoot Way and turn left walking to the next corner to another traffic light.
23. At the traffic light turn right onto Crowfoot Circle and follow it past a traffic circle and the bus stop area.
24. Cross the overpass back to the station.

Crowfoot Walk Two
Bowmont Park West, Baker Park
& Bowness Park

Walk Overview: This linear route starts at the station. After a short section in Scenic Acres the route enters Silver Springs and follows a paved path down through the west ravine of Bowmont Park. From the bottom end of the ravine the route follows the Bow River Pathway west to Baker Park and then crosses the river to Bowness Park. Bowness is one of Calgary's older communities with the village of Bowness first being settled in 1911. Although the village was annexed by Calgary in 1964 the community has retained some small town or village ambience. Some parts of this route are isolated so use your own discretion about walking alone.

Length: 9.5 km

Route Description & Accessibility: Accessibility could be challenging on the long descent through the ravine. There is no suitable detour included in the text. Most of the remainder of the route is relatively flat. The walking surface for most of the route is paved paths or sidewalks with short sections on trails in each of the three parks.

Food and Drink: There are benches in Baker Park and picnic tables in Bowness Park. Near the start of this route you pass a convenience store and a pizza outlet. Near the bus stop on 85th Street at the end of the route there is a restaurant and a small rather charming hamburger café. There is also a café in Bowness Park. As part of the renovations in the park a new restaurant will replace the building where the café is located. There are also restaurants and coffee shops near the station.

Washrooms: Baker Park has a seasonal washroom building. There are several washroom buildings in Bowness Park.

Map References: Clear-View – 7 & 15, MapArt – 143 & 153 Rand McNally – 23, Sherlock – 8, 16 & 15

Route Category: Walk/Bus – The route starts from the station. At the end of the walk ride the bus back to the station.

The Walk: At the upper level of the station building turn left and cross the pedestrian overpass to the south side of Crowchild Trail into the community of Scenic Acres. This overpass ends at ground level. Turn right and follow the sidewalk towards the Crowfoot Parade Bridge. Make a left turn and follow the sidewalk past the parking lot to where Crowchild Parade ends at Scurfield Drive (0.4 km). Follow Scurfield Drive to the left as it bends right and heads south to a traffic light at Scenic Acres Boulevard. Turn left and follow Scenic Acres Boulevard east to the traffic light on Nose Hill Drive (1.1 km).

Cross to the east side of Nose Hill Drive and turn right walking south past Spring Hill Village shopping centre to the traffic light at Silver Springs Boulevard. Turn left on Silver Springs Boulevard and walk east to Silver Grove Drive at the next corner. Turn right and walk south on Silver Grove Drive past the Silver Heights condo complex on the left. On the south side of the condos there is a large green space on the left just beyond Silverthorn Drive. Look for a path leading to the left through the green space. The route now begins a long descent. The path heads south past Silverview Point housing complex on the left. Cross Silver Springs Road at the pedestrian crossing (2.3 km). On the south side of the road follow the path down into the west ravine of Bowmont Park.

The site of Bowmont Park was once part of the Cochrane Ranche property, the first of many large ranches in Western Canada. The company leased over one hundred thousand acres. The first cattle were purchased in 1881. Matthew H. Cochrane of Quebec was the president of the company. Bowmont Park is a large natural area stretching along the flood plain, escarpment slope and plateau on the south side of Silver Springs and Varsity Estates. The west boundary is 85th Street. The east boundary is 53rd Street and 40th Avenue in the northeast corner and 32nd Avenue and Home Road in the southeast corner. The park name derives from combining the first syllables of Bowness and Montgomery communities. The community of Silver Springs is named after a location in Florida.

The route down through the ravine is very pleasant. In the colder months of the year the path may be icy or snow covered. At the bottom end of the ravine a trail leading down some steps on the right from Silver Valley Boulevard joins the path. On the left a path leading down the side of the ravine from Silver Crest Drive joins the path (3.3 km). Continue on the main path past these two junctions. At the next junction take the left branch. The right branch path leads to a parking lot at the west end of the park. The route then passes a fenced off area with storm ponds built to collect water during heavy rainfalls. On the left as you pass by the storm ponds is the former property of the Fournier family who lived in this area for many years. The city purchased the property in 2000. The house was severely vandalized and had to be demolished. A trail leads off the path to a wetlands fed by an underground spring.

After exploring the Fournier Trail continue on the main path towards the large black railway bridge (3.6 km). After passing under the bridge the route reaches a major trail junction. Turn left and cross a small bridge onto an island. Follow the path across the island to the larger Bowmont Bridge for pedestrians on the south side of the island (3.9 km). East of this bridge is the second train bridge. Retrace your steps back across the island and the small bridge to the main path.

Turn left and follow the path west passing under 85th Street Bridge (4.7 km). On the west side of the bridge continue west along the riverbank past the south side of Bow Park Court and enter the east end of Baker Park (5.1 km). The park stretches along the north side of the Bow River west of Bow Park Court. Baker Park is the park you can see when standing by the river in Bowness Park and looking across to the far bank.

The park is located on the former site of the Baker Memorial Sanatorium buildings. The sanatorium served as a treatment centre for tuberculosis patients from 1920 to the 1970s. The centre's namesake, Dr. A.H. Baker, was the sanatorium's director from 1920 to 1950. The facility was later used as a treatment centre for children and adults before the buildings were demolished in the 1980s.

The park is divided into areas with charming names such as: The Commons, Wildflower Mount, The Sunbowl and Scenic Bow Arbour. The main path along the riverbank leads you to The Sunbowl area of the park. On the east and west sides of The Sunbowl are two bronze sculptures of bear cubs entitled *Twin Bears* and *Playful Cubs* by artist Leo Mol. Follow the path as it curves around the north side of The Sunbowl. On the right is the parking lot for Baker Park. The washroom building is on the west side of the parking lot (5.5 km).

Aerial view of Central Alberta Sanatorium, Calgary ca. 1940s. Glenbow Archives NA-2910-9. On the far side of the river is Bowness Park

West of the washroom building you can do a bit of exploring amongst the trees. In this area you can see the remains of the old sidewalks that connected the Baker Sanatorium buildings. One circular section of sidewalk surrounds a group of trees. After your exploring retrace your steps back to the main path by the river and continue westbound. As the path leaves Baker Park it curves away from the river and continues around the north side of a city water pumping station. The path then passes under Stoney Trail Bridge before making a loop to the left to reach the pedestrian bridge underneath Stoney Trail Bridge (7.0 km). On your right as you make the loop is the east fence of the Al Azhar Shrine Temple property.

At the far end of the bridge you enter the west end of Bowness Park. At the time of writing the park is undergoing major renovations so you may have to detour around construction sites. In 1908 John Hextall, an Englishman, purchased the Bowness Ranch and built a mansion for his family. Wood's Christian Home became a later occupant of the building. Hextall planned to attract wealthy settlers from Great Britain by selling lots with the requirement that the homes had to be worth at least $3,500. The

Old sidewalk remains in Baker Park

collapse of the real estate market resulted in just a few of these homes being built. In 1911 Bowness was connected to Calgary with a bridge through an agreement made with the city whereby Hextall donated the bridge and land for a city park in exchange for the city providing regular streetcar service from the bridge to the park.

Canoeing in the park started in 1918. In the 1920s numerous facilities were added to the park including a picnic pavilion, a swimming pool, a merry-go-round (this is now in Heritage Park), summer cottages that visitors could rent, a dance hall and a concession. Later additions to the park were a shooting gallery, a miniature railway, pony rides and some amusement park rides. The first fountain in the lagoon operated from 1927 until the late 1960s. The Parks Department installed the present fountain in 1988. By the 1940s the cottages were demolished. The pool closed in 1959 and this was followed by the closure of the dance hall the following year.

The renovations planned include the building of one large parking lot near the entrance, a children's water park and a new building with food facilities. The remnants of the amusement park and the mini-golf have been removed to enlarge the parking area.

The route turns left from the bridge and follows the south bank of the river to the 85th Street end of the park. Bowness Park has been one of Calgary's most popular family parks for many years. In the warmer weather hundreds of people congregate here beside the Bow River for picnics. There are several picnic shelters that can be reserved by groups. Numerous barbeque stands and fire pits are scattered throughout the park. Park users in the summer months can choose from a wide variety of activities. You can rent one of the paddleboats or canoes and explore the lagoon or canal. A spray pool area is also very popular on hot summer days. There are also open grass areas for impromptu ball games or a game of croquet or bocce. In the winter large numbers of visitors head for the park for an enjoyable afternoon of skating around the lagoon and then huddling around one of the fire pits to warm up. Walk 3 – West Bowness and Valley Ridge Escarpment in this chapter also visits the park.

At the 85th Street end of the park you angle to the right and follow a path up to 85th Street (9.1 km). Walk south on 85th Street to 48th Avenue. Cross to the southeast corner of the intersection and walk south to the end of the route at 46th Avenue (9.5 km).

Boating at Bowness Park, 1922. Glenbow Archives NA-1496-4

Bus Directions from the end of the route to the station: Catch bus # 40 Crowfoot at stop 6731 on northbound 85th Street at 46th Avenue. Get off the bus at stop 3858 back at the station. The scheduled time back to the station is 12 minutes. The bus frequency is 35 minutes daily.

Route Summary:

1. From the upper level of the station building turn left and cross the pedestrian overpass to the south side of Crowchild Trail in the community of Scenic Acres.
2. Turn right and follow the sidewalk to Crowfoot Parade Bridge.
3. Make a left turn and follow the sidewalk past the parking lot to where Crowfoot Parade ends at Scurfield Drive.
4. Follow Scurfield Drive to the left as it bends right and heads south to a traffic light at Scenic Acres Boulevard.
5. Turn left and walk east on Scenic Acres Boulevard to Nose Hill Drive.
6. Cross to the east side of Nose Hill Drive at the traffic light, turn right and walk south to the traffic light at Silver Springs Boulevard.
7. Turn left on Silver Springs Boulevard and then turn right onto Silver Grove Drive.
8. As you reach a large green space on your left follow a path leading downhill through the green space.
9. Cross Silver Springs Road at the pedestrian crossing and follow the path south as it descends through the west ravine of Bowmont Park.
10. Continue straight ahead at the next two junctions as a trail and then a path lead down the slope to join your path near the bottom of the ravine.
11. At the third junction take the left branch past the storm pond.
12. Follow a trail to the left to visit the Fournier Trail. Return to the path and continue on the main path as it heads towards a large black train bridge.
13. Walk under the bridge and turn left across a small bridge onto an island.
14. Follow the path across the island to Bowmont Bridge.
15. Retrace your steps back to the path west of the train bridge and turn left.
16. Follow the path as it heads west passing under the 85th Street Bridge.
17. On the west side of the bridge continue west past Bow Park Court and enter the east side of Baker Park.
18. Follow the path to The Sunbowl area of Baker Park.
19. Follow the curved path around the north side of The Sunbowl and turn right into the parking lot.
20. Turn left and follow a path from the parking lot towards the washroom building.
21. Explore for old sidewalks in the treed area on the west side of the

washroom building before returning to the main path by the river and continuing west.

22. After leaving Baker Park the path curves to the right away from the river passing by the north side of a city water pumping station.
23. The path passes under Stoney Trail Bridge and makes a loop to the left to reach the pedestrian bridge under Stoney Trail Bridge.
24. At the far end of the bridge you enter Bowness Park. Turn left and follow the trail beside the river.
25. This trail leads to the 85th Street end of Bowness Park.
26. Angle to the right as you near the bridge and follow a path up to 85th Street.
27. Turn right and walk south on 85th Street to a four-way stop at 48th Avenue.
28. Cross to the southeast corner of the intersection and walk south on 85th Street to the bus stop near 46th Avenue.
29. Catch bus # 40 Crowfoot at stop 6731. Get off the bus at stop 3858 back at the station.

Crowfoot Walk Three
West Bowness &
Valley Ridge Escarpment

Walk Overview: This route is a mix of out-and-back and linear sections. In the first half of the route you follow the canal along the south side of Bowness Park and climbs the steep escarpment slope to the north side of Valley Ridge. At the time of writing Bowness Park is undergoing a major restoration. You may have to detour around construction sites until the restoration is completed. After descending the escarpment you complete the route by making a loop along several streets at the west end of Bowness passing several older homes and an older school building. Parts of the escarpment are a bit isolated so use your discretion about visiting this area on your own.

Length: 8.7 km

Route Description & Accessibility: The Bowness Park and West Bowness sections of this route have good accessibility. As you enter Bowness Park there is a short downhill section on the access road into the park. The walking surface in the park is a mix of paved paths and a cinder trail. As you leave the park there is a short uphill on the access road.

Accessibility on the Valley Ridge escarpment slope is very poor. No alternate route is included in the text.

Food and Drink: Bowness Park has many picnic tables. On 85th Street south of 48th Avenue there is a restaurant and a small rather charming hamburger café. There are also restaurants and coffee shops near the station.

Washrooms: There are several washroom buildings in Bowness Park.

Map References: Clear-View – 15 & 68, MapArt – 153 & 152
Rand McNally – 35 & 34, Sherlock - 16 & 15

Route Category: Bus/Walk/Bus – Ride the bus to the start of the route and when finished the walk ride the bus back to the station.

Bus Directions from the station to the start of the walk: At the upper level of the station building turn right and cross the pedestrian overpass above Crowchild Trail to the bus stop area. Catch bus # 40 North Hill at stop 3858. Get off at stop 6739 on southbound 85th Street just south of 48th Avenue. This stop is 17 minutes from the station. The bus frequency is 35 minutes daily.

The Walk: After getting off the bus walk back to the corner of 48th Avenue and 85th Street, turn left and head west on 48th Avenue. After one block you reach the access road into Bowness Park (0.3 km). In this block two older homes built in 1912 date back to the era of John Hextall.

Follow the access road down into Bowness Park and cross a bridge. The lagoon is on the right and the canal is on the left. In the summer months canoeists and paddle-boaters paddle around the lagoon or follow the canal to the west end of the park. In the winter skaters populate the lagoon and canal surfaces. The concession building is just to the right of the access road beside a parking lot and the lagoon. On the west wall of the concession building is a large mural depicting Bowness Park in the summer and in the winter. As part of the park renovations this mural will probably disappear when the concession building is replaced by a newer structure. A washroom building is also nearby. You can spend a few minutes exploring the area on your right adjacent to the lagoon. On the far side of the parking lot a paved path crosses a bridge over a small water canal where the rental canoes and paddleboats are kept. The other side of the bridge is a small island with another bridge at the east end crossing over the small canal (0.7 km). There is an information plaque beside the path outlining the history of the Bowness Park Lagoon Fountain.

Retrace your steps back to the parking lot. Go to the right around the north side of the concession building and past the washroom building to where you cross the access road onto a cinder trail beside the canal (1.0 km). Follow this trail along the edge of the canal to the west end of the park.

Mural depicting Bowness Park in the winter

The trail ends by the south end of Stoney Trail pedestrian bridge (2.2 km). Walk 2 – Bowmont Park West, Baker Park and Bowness Park passes through this area crossing Stoney Trail pedestrian bridge and turning left to follow the river bank along the north side of the park.

There is one short trail to explore before you climb the escarpment slope up to Valley Ridge. Turn left at the west end of the canal and make another left turn onto a trail on the south side of the canal. This area, called the Wood's Douglas Fir Tree Sanctuary, has some trees over 400 years old. The location was designated as a provincial historic resource in 1990. The trail is not well developed and soon ends. The distance walked on this trail is not included in the length of this walk.

After exploring this trail and retracing your steps to the bridge follow the paved path that switchbacks up the escarpment below Stoney Trail Bridge. At the top of the escarpment you are at the northeast corner of the community of Valley Ridge. Follow the path along the top of the escarpment until it reaches a turn around point where the path turns left to go between houses to Valley Springs Road. Retrace your route back along the path until you reach a trail with numerous stairs that descends the escarpment slope back to the bridge (4.9 km). Follow the trail down the slope back to the bridge.

Retrace your route back along the canal and follow the access road out of the park to 48th Avenue (6.1 km). Turn right and head west towards the end of 48th Avenue. In the 8900 block you pass an older home built in 1912. The Bowness Ranch House constructed in the early 1890s and demolished in the late 1950s was just west of the access road into the park. The Hextall family lived here from 1910 until 1912 before building their large new home at the west end of 48th Avenue.

When the route reaches the west end of 48th Avenue you will be standing in front of the gateway for the George Wood Centre (6.6 km). Just beyond where you are standing was the location of the Hextall Mansion built in 1911-12. In 1916, after the death of John Hextall, the house was sold. The building was briefly used as an auto clubhouse and then used as a sanatorium before becoming the Woods Christian Home in 1926. The Hextall Mansion was torn down after a fire in 1975.

Retrace your steps back a short distance along 48th Avenue past a small

Alberta Sanatorium, ca. 1917-1919. Glenbow Archives NA-2133-8

playground on the right and turn right onto 34th Avenue. On this first block the route passes two older homes dating back to 1912 during the era of John Hextall. Turn right at 88th Street and at the next corner turn left onto 33rd Avenue (7.1 km).

Follow this road southeast to 83rd Street where you turn left and walk one block north. On the northeast corner is St. Edmund's Anglican Church (8.0 km). This church was built in 1949. St. Edmund the Martyr, King of East Anglia, was born about 840 and died in 870.

Turn left and walk west on 34th Avenue. Turn right at 85th Street and head north to where 85th Street meets Bowness Road. A barrier blocks traffic between Bowness Road and 85th Street south of Bowness Road. On the left is the former Bowness School building built in the 1930s. Continue north on 85th Street to 46th Avenue. Cross to the northeast corner of the intersection to the end of the route (8.7 km).

Bus Directions from the end of the route to the station: Catch bus # 40 Crowfoot at stop 6731 on northbound 85th Street at 46th Avenue. Get off the bus at stop 3858 back at the station. The scheduled time back to the station is 12 minutes. The bus frequency is 35 minutes daily.

Route Summary:

1. From the upper level of the station turn right and cross the pedestrian overpass to the north side of Crowchild Trail.
2. Catch bus # 40 North Hill at stop 3858. Get off the bus at stop 6739 on southbound 85th Street just south of 48th Avenue.
3. After getting off the bus walk back to the corner of 85th Street and 48th Avenue and turn left.
4. Walk west one block to the access road into Bowness Road.
5. Follow the road into the park crossing a bridge over the park canal.
6. Angle to the right across a parking lot and cross a smaller bridge onto a small island adjacent to the canoe rentals area.
7. Retrace your steps back to the parking lot and walk past a washroom building and cross the access road to reach a trail beside the canal.
8. Follow the trail to the west end of the park below Stoney Trail Bridge.
9. Turn left at the west end of the canal and make another left turn onto a trail on the south side of the canal.
10. After exploring this trail retrace your steps to the bridge and follow the paved path that switchbacks up the escarpment below Stoney Trail Bridge.
11. Follow the path along the top of the escarpment until it reaches the

turn around point where the path turns left to go between houses to Valley Springs Road.

12. Retrace your route back along the path turning left onto a trail that descends numerous stairs on the escarpment slope back to the bridge.
13. Retrace your route back through the park to 48th Avenue.
14. Turn right and walk west to the end of 48th Avenue.
15. Retrace your route back along 48th Avenue and turn right onto 34th Avenue.
16. Turn right at 88th Street and left at 33rd Avenue.
17. Follow 33rd Avenue east to 83rd Street.
18. Turn left and walk one block north to 34th Avenue.
19. Walk west on 34th Avenue to 85th Street.
20. Walk north on 85th Street to 46th Avenue.
21. Cross to the northeast corner at the end of the walk.
22. Catch bus # 40 Crowfoot at stop 6731. Get off at stop 3858 back at the station.

Crowfoot Walk Four
Bow Crescent & Bowness Road

Walk Overview: The first section of this route passes through the undeveloped part of Bowness Park east of 85th Street. This section of the route is a bit isolated so use your own discretion about walking alone. From here the route goes under the CPR Bridge and follows Bow Crescent all the way to James Hextall Bridge. The first section of Bow Crescent is rather like walking down a country lane with no sidewalks and some houses hidden amongst the trees. The last section of the route follows Bowness Road from James Hextall Bridge west to 77th Street. Bowness Road has a variety of shops and businesses.

Length: 7.7 km

Route Description & Accessibility: This route is relatively flat. The only poor accessibility is in the section of Bowness Park east of 85th Street where the walking surface is uneven dirt trails. Information on a detour route is included in the text. The road surface on some sections of Bow Crescent can be a bit uneven.

Food and Drink: On the second half of the walk you pass convenience stores, coffee shops and restaurants along Bowness Road and also west of 77th Street near the end of the route. There are also restaurants and coffee shops near the station.

Washrooms: There are several washroom buildings in Bowness Park. Near the halfway point of the walk you can cross John Hextall Bridge and use the washrooms in Shouldice Park or at Shouldice Indoor Swimming Pool.

Map References: Clear-View – 15 & 16, MapArt – 153
Rand McNally – 35 & 36, Sherlock – 16 & 17

Route Category: Bus/Walk/Bus – Ride the bus to the start of the route and when finished the walk ride the bus back to the station.

Bus Directions from the station to the start of the walk: At the upper level of the station building turn right and cross the pedestrian overpass above Crowchild Trail to the bus stop area. Catch bus # 40 North Hill at stop 3858. Get off at stop 6739 on southbound 85th Street just south of 48th Avenue. This stop is 17 minutes from the station. The bus frequency is 35 minutes daily.

The Walk: After getting off the bus walk back to the corner of 85th Street and 48th Avenue. Cross to the northeast corner of the intersection and walk down the slope on 85th Street heading towards the bridge. Before reaching the bridge, turn right and follow a paved path down into the east end of Bowness Park. This portion of the park is a natural area with no

Small bridge at east end of Bowness Park

development except for a few dirt trails.

Continue straight ahead on the path to reach the trail by the river. Turn right and follow this trail to the east end of the natural area. The trail will bend to the right, cross a small wooden bridge (0.7 km) and climb up a short incline into a small park . Follow the trail to the south side of the park to 48th Avenue across from Bowness Baptist Church.

Turn left and follow 48th Avenue east to just beyond 79th Street where you follow a path on the left down a set of stairs between houses. The path leads to Bowmont Bridge (1.2 km). To avoid the dirt trails and the stairs walk east on 48th Avenue from the corner at 85th Street and turn left onto Bow Green Crescent. A path at the far end of this street will lead to the riverbank near the bridge.

From Bowmont Bridge, walk east on the path going underneath the south end of the railway bridge. On your right behind the wire fence next to the railway tracks are some wooden stairs that are obviously not used anymore. What was the original use of these stairs? On the far side of the bridge the path turns right and leads to the end of Bow Village Crescent on the left and to Bow Crescent on the right. Follow Bow Crescent east to where it turns

Old stairs behind the railway fence

right and heads southeast. There are no sidewalks on this section of Bow Crescent. The homes on the right back onto the railway tracks and the homes on the left back onto the Bow River.

At 67th Street Bow Crescent makes a slight turn to the left and continues in a southeasterly direction (2.7 km). There is a small park on the left near 66th Street with access to the river. Just east of 61st Street the road makes another slight turn to the left and then makes a large loop to the right beyond 59th Street. This turn will lead you to a small park at the west end of John Hextall Bridge. Bow Crescent ends at Bowness Road (4.8 km). John Hextall Bridge, constructed in 1910-11, is located north of Shouldice Bridge that was constructed in the 1980s. The Municipal Railway started using the bridge in 1912 to cross the river on the way to Bowness Park. James Hextall had made arrangements with the city that he would build the bridge and donate the land for Bowness Park if the city extended the street railway line to the west end of Bowness.

The land for Shouldice Park on the far side of the bridge was a gift to the city in the 1910s from James Shouldice and his neighbour Alfred S. McKay. They donated 100 acres for use as a park. There are several information plaques on the bridge. James and Mary Shouldice and their family settled in Calgary in 1901. Their family home overlooked the Bow River at the top of Home Road. Later the building was used as a crematorium. On Lions Park Walk 2 – 29th Street to Shouldice Park there is a short detour on 37th Street to view the Alfred McKay house. McKay worked as a ferryman on the Centre Street crossing of the Bow River. MacKay Road (note the spelling difference) on the east side of Montgomery is named for Alfred McKay. Point McKay housing complex is also named for him.

From James Hextall Bridge you head north on Bowness Road. At 60th Street Bowness Road turns left and heads northwest through the commercial area of the community with retail stores, restaurants and other businesses lining both sides of the street. The route leaves the retail section just beyond 65th Street. At 67th Street Bowness Road turns slightly to the left and goes under the CPR tracks (6.5 km).

At 77th Street there is a strip mall on the northwest corner of the intersection. Turn left and walk north on 77th Street to view two artistic points of interests located on the side of buildings on the west side of 77th Street north of Bowness Road. The first location has jigsaw-like pieces arranged in circles on the side of a building. The second piece of art is a mural of Bowness Park on the side of a building. Queen Elizabeth Park is on the north side of 41st Avenue east of 77th Street across from the strip mall (7.5 km). The park has a memorial stone dedicated to the memory of those who gave their lives in military service. In the northwest corner of the park is a second stone with a plaque to commemorate the coronation of Queen

Elizabeth in 1953.

Bus Directions from the end of the route back to the station: From the park walk a few steps north to the bus stop. Catch bus # 40 Crowfoot at stop 4062. Get off the bus at stop 3858 at the station. The scheduled time back to the station is 15 minutes. The bus frequency is 35 minutes daily.

Route Summary:

1. From the upper level of the station turn right and cross the pedestrian overpass to the north side of Crowchild Trail.
2. Catch bus # 40 North Hill at stop 3858. Get off the bus at stop 6739 on southbound 85th Street just south of 48th Avenue.
3. Walk back to the corner of 85th Street and 48th Avenue and cross to the northeast corner.
4. Start walking downhill towards the bridge and turn right onto a path.
5. When the path reaches a trail beside the river turn right on the trail.
6. Follow the trail crossing a small bridge and ascend a small slope in a

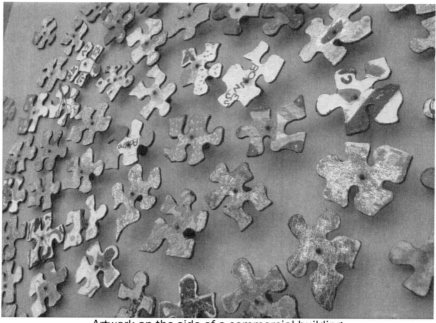

Artwork on the side of a commercial building
on 77th Street north of Bowness Road.

park to reach 48th Avenue.

7. Turn left on 48th Avenue and just beyond 79th Street turn left down a short set of stairs to follow a path between houses.
8. The path leads to Bowmont Bridge.
9. Continue on the path going underneath the train bridge.
10. The path leads to where Bow Village Crescent on the left meets Bow Crescent on the right.
11. Follow Bow Crescent east and then south.
12. At 67th Street continue on Bow Crescent as it turns left.
13. Just after 61st Street the road angles to the left and then makes a large loop to the right that leads to a park beside John Hextall Bridge.
14. From the bridge walk north on Bowness Road.
15. At 60th Street Bowness Road turns left and heads northwest.
16. Just beyond 67th Street Bowness Road goes under the railway tracks.
17. Turn right at 77th Street and walk north to a bus stop just north of 41st Avenue.
18. Catch bus # 40 Crowfoot at stop 4062 on northbound 77th Street north of 41st Avenue. Get off the bus at stop 3858 back at the station.

Crowfoot Walk Five
Scenic Acres

Walk Overview: Most of this out-and-back route follows a paved path through a shallow ravine to the turn around point at the tunnel leading under Stoney Trail into Twelve Mile Coulee. Depending on the time of year water may be flowing through the ravine.

Length: 6.4 km

Route Description & Accessibility: The walking surface for most of the route is paved paths with some walking on grass or sidewalks. Information on a detour route for the grass is included in the text. On the first half of the route you are going gradually downhill and then change to a gradual uphill on the second half of the route. Some of the descents and ascents are a bit steeper.

Food and Drink: There are no food stores or restaurants along the route.

Washrooms: There are no public washrooms along the route.

Map References: Clear-View – 7, MapArt – 143
Rand McNally – 23, Sherlock – 8, 16

Route Category: Walk – The route starts and ends at the station (no bus is required).

The Walk: From the upper level of the station turn left and cross the pedestrian overpass to the south side of Crowchild Trail. Turn right and walk a few steps to the south end of Crowfoot Parade overpass (the road that crosses over Crowchild Trail just west of the station).

Turn left and follow the edge of Crowfoot Parade to Scurfield Drive (0.4 km). Turn right and walk west along Scurfield Drive. As you pass the Scenic Acres Community Hall on the left, turn and walk south passing between the hall and Monsignor Doyle School. Edwin Lawrence Doyle, a native of Prince Edward Island, taught at St. Mary's High School from 1919 until his appointment as acting principal in 1938. Bishop McNally ordained Doyle in 1922. Doyle served as parish priest at St. Anne's Church in Ramsay from 1938 until his death in 1959. Pope Pius XII raised him to the dignity of Monsignor in 1957.

After passing the school and the hall angle to the right and walk past Scenic Acres School keeping the school on the left. Walk southwest across the grass towards the farthest houses on Scenic Hill Close.

Boardwalk along Scenic Acres Pathway

169

When you reach Scenic Acres Boulevard beside the last house, step over the wire strung between posts along the edge of the field (1.3 km) and walk a few steps to your right to the corner where Scenic Acres Gate heads south from Scenic Acres Boulevard. If you require better accessibility than the grass follow Scurfield Way south from the parking lot for Monsignor Doyle School and turn right on Scenic Acres Boulevard walking west to rejoin the route at Scenic Acres Gate.

Cross to the south side of Scenic Acres Boulevard and follow the path south along the west side of Scenic Acres Gate to a t-intersection with Scenic Park Crescent (1.5 km). Cross this road and follow the path south down a gradual slope into a shallow ravine. The area on both sides of the path is mostly covered in trees and shrubs. At a trail junction by a boardwalk, keep to the left and at the next junction take the right branch. The path leads to a more open area with a good view to the south and southwest. The houses at the south end of Scenic Glen Crescent are on the left. As the path heads down another gradual slope you pass playing fields, a playground and tennis courts.

The path ends on the north side of Scenic Acres Drive (2.3 km). Turn left and walk a few steps east to the corner at Scimitar Point. Cross to the south side of Scenic Acres Drive and turn right. Walk west a few steps to where the

Water flowing through Scenic Acres Ravine

path starts again on the south side of Scenic Acres Drive. Note that there is no crosswalk on Scenic Acres Drive where the path ends. On the south side of the road follow the path as it continues south. Ignore any paths branching off from the main path. Depending on the time of year there may be a small stream of water flowing through this area. The path then turns to the right and heads west. On the right are the houses on Scenic Ridge Crescent and on the left the houses on Scimitar Point. At a four-way junction keep going straight ahead (2.7 km). The turn around point is when the path reaches the east end of a tunnel under Stoney Trail (3.2 km). At the time of writing there is a large construction project on the west side of Stoney Trail building an overpass to allow for a free flow of traffic on Stoney Trail. From the tunnel turn around and retrace your route back to the station (6.4 km).

Route Summary:
1. From the upper level of the station turn left and cross the pedestrian overpass to the south side of Crowchild Trail.
2. Turn right and follow the sidewalk to the south end of Crowfoot Parade Bridge.
3. Turn left and follow Crowchild Parade south to Scurfield Drive.
4. Turn right and walk west on Scurfield Drive to the Scenic Acres Community Hall on the left.
5. Turn left and walk south between the hall on the left and Monsignor Doyle School on the right.
6. Angle to the right keeping Scenic Acres School on the left and walk southwest across the playing field to the far corner where you reach Scenic Acres Boulevard.
7. Turn right walking west on Scenic Acres Boulevard and turn left onto Scenic Acres Gate.
8. Walk south to a T-intersection with Scenic Park Crescent.
9. Continue straight ahead following a path down a gradual slope into a shallow ravine.
10. Stay left at the first junction.
11. At the next junction stay right.
12. When the path ends at Scenic Acres Drive turn left and walk a few steps to Scimitar Point.
13. Cross this road and walk a few steps west to where the path starts.
14. Follow the path south and then west.
14. At a four-way junction go straight ahead.
15. The path leads to a tunnel under Stoney Trail.
16. From the tunnel retrace your route back to the station.

Chapter Nine
Tuscany Station

Station Information: At the time of writing the track extension from Crowfoot Station to Tuscany Station is still under construction. The walk directions described in the text are from the location of Tuscany Station. For the four walks listed in this chapter temporary bus directions between Crowfoot Station and bus stops in Tuscany or Royal Oak are included for the starting and finishing locations of the four walks prior to Tuscany Station opening. Most of the temporary starting and finishing points for the four walks are different from the start and finish points that will be used after Tuscany Station opens. When Tuscany Station opens in 2014 all four walks will start and finish at the station. No buses will be required for the four walks. The temporary bus directions from Crowfoot Station and the temporary starting and finishing points will no longer be needed.

In the summer of 2012 work began on Tuscany Station and the pedestrian overpasses above Crowchild Trail. The station is in the centre median of Crowchild Trail. On the north side of Crowchild Trail the closest intersection is where Eamon Road joins Rocky Ridge Road. On the south side of Crowchild Trail the closest road is Tuscany Springs Boulevard near The Mosaic and Sierras of Tuscany condo buildings.

Tuscany community was developed in the 1990s. Development of the communities of Royal Oak and Rocky Ridge started in the late 1990s after the area had been annexed by the city in 1989. The name Twelve Mile Coulee dates back before the development of the nearby residential communities. Twelve Mile Coulee Road on the west side of Tuscany and Rocky Ridge was named for the twelve miles distance from the city centre.

Tuscany Walk One
Twelve Mile Coulee

Walk Overview: This out-and-back route follows paved paths and sidewalks from Tuscany Station to the path along the top of the escarpment above Twelve Mile Coulee. About 600 metres along this path you follow a dirt trail down into the bottom of the coulee. At the turn around point you retrace your steps back along the same route. The coulee is an excellent natural park with water sometimes trickling through the area. The vegetation on the sides of the ravines ranges from open areas to heavily treed. At the time of writing there is ongoing construction near the bottom end of the ravine for the interchange of Stoney Trail and Nose Hill Drive. Please note that the trail through the bottom of the ravine is isolated so use your own discretion about walking alone.

Length: 7.6 km

Route Description & Accessibility: The accessibility for this route is very poor. The walking surface in the coulee is very uneven and often muddy. No alternate route is included in the text.

Food and Drink: There are no stores, coffee shops or restaurants along this route.

Washrooms: There are no public washrooms along this route.

Map References: Clear-View – 1 & A16, MapArt – 142 & 143 Rand McNally – 22, Sherlock – 7 & 15

Route Category: Walk – The route starts and ends at Tuscany Station.

The Walk: From the upper level of Tuscany Station use the pedestrian overpass to cross to the south side of Crowchild Trail into the community of Tuscany. Follow the parking lot access road to where it meets Tuscany Springs Boulevard. Cross to the far side of the road and turn left heading south along the west side of Tuscany Springs Boulevard. Follow Tuscany Springs Boulevard until it meets Tuscany Boulevard at a traffic light intersection (1.2 km). Please note that this intersection will be the starting point for the walk until Tuscany Station opens.

Temporary Bus Directions from Crowfoot Station to the temporary start of the walk: Catch bus # 74 Tuscany at stop 9879. Get off at stop 8432 on northbound Tuscany Springs Boulevard just north of Tuscany Boulevard. This stop is 9 minutes from Crowfoot Station. The bus frequency is 45 minutes daily. From this bus stop follow the directions listed below until you reach the bus stop where you return to Crowfoot Station.

Cross to the south side of Tuscany Boulevard and turn right following the path west to another traffic light intersection. At this corner Tuscany Valley View leads north on the right and Tuscany Hills Road leads south on the left.

Make a turn to the left and start to follow the path leading along the upper edge of the coulee (1.5 km). At this point the coulee is very shallow. This section of path is also on Walk 2 – Tuscany Escarpment. After about 600 metres you reach a rest area with a carved buffalo sculpture entitled *Sunning Buffalo* by Eric Peterson (2.1 km). From here the route descends down the slope to the bottom of the coulee. The descent has pieces of wood inserted into the ground at right angles to your direction of travel to serve as a primitive set of stairs. Within the coulee there are places where the trail

Trail through Twelve Mile Coulee

splits along the bottom and sometimes traverses the slope on the east side of the coulee.

The trail through the coulee can be muddy. Pick your own route depending on the trail conditions. You will probably have to cross the water several times. Sometimes the trail passes through wooded areas and at times the coulee is more open with fewer trees and bushes. As the route nears the bottom of the ravine there is an excellent view of Stoney Trail Bridge.

When the route nears the point where the construction area for the interchange is on the left and the escarpment slope on the right turns west away from you it is time to turn around (3.8 km). When the construction is finished it will be easier to reach the turn around point of Crowfoot Walk 5 – Scenic Acres at the other end of the tunnel on the east side of Stoney Trail. After turning around retrace your same route back to Tuscany Station (7.6 km). The temporary route ends at the intersection of Tuscany Boulevard at Tuscany Hills Road.

Temporary Bus Directions from the temporary end of the walk back to Crowfoot Station: After retracing your route back through the coulee, catch bus # 74 Tuscany at stop 8003 on eastbound Tuscany Boulevard at Tuscany

Hills Road. Get off at stop 9879 back at the station. The scheduled time back to Crowfoot Station is 12 minutes. The bus frequency is 45 minutes daily.

Route Summary: (the temporary bus directions from Crowfoot Station are not included in this summary).

1. From the upper level of Tuscany Station use the pedestrian overpass to reach the south side of Crowchild Trail.
2. Follow the edge of the parking lot to Tuscany Springs Boulevard.
3. Cross to the far side of the road and turn left on the west side of Tuscany Springs Boulevard walking south to traffic lights at Tuscany Boulevard. This is the temporary starting point until Tuscany Station is open.
4. Cross to the south side of Tuscany Boulevard and turn right walking west to the traffic lights at Tuscany Hills Road.
5. Turn left and follow the path behind the houses along the upper edge of the coulee.
6. At the rest area with the buffalo sculpture descend the slope to the bottom of the coulee.
7. Turn right and follow the trail through the coulee. At times you may have to choose your own route if the trail is too muddy.
8. When you reach the bottom end of the ravine turn around and retrace your route back to the station. The temporary route ends at Tuscany Boulevard and Tuscany Hills Road intersection where you catch bus # 74 Tuscany at stop 8003 back to Crowfoot Station.

Tuscany Walk Two
Tuscany Escarpment

Walk Overview: This route follows paved paths along the top of the escarpments located on the south and east sides of Tuscany. For almost the entire route you have excellent views of the Bow Valley. The first and last 1.4 km of the route is an out-and-back section. The remaining portion of the route is a large loop.

Length: 10.8 km

Route Description & Accessibility: Almost the entire section along the top of the escarpment is relatively flat with good accessibility. There are some sections along the route where the ascent or descent can be less accessible. Information about detours for these sections is included in the text. There are other sections with more gradual descents or ascents.

Food and Drink: In the first 2 km of the route you pass Tuscany Market shopping centre.

Washrooms: There are no public washrooms along the route.

Map References: Clear-View – A16, MapArt – 142 & 143
Rand McNally – 22, Sherlock – 7 & 15

Route Category: Walk – The route starts and ends at Tuscany Station (no bus is required).

The Walk: From the upper level of Tuscany Station turn left and cross the pedestrian overpass to the south side of Crowchild Trail. Follow the access road for the station parking lot to where it meets Tuscany Springs Boulevard. Cross to the far side of the road and turn left on a path that heads south from the Sierras of Tuscany condos. At a junction turn right and follow a path west across a playing field to the top of a slope looking west. At the next junction turn left following the path as it angles down the slope towards Tuscany Valley View. When the path reaches the bottom of the slope (0.9 km) turn left and follow the path south on a gradual descent beside Tuscany Valley View to the intersection where it meets Tuscany Boulevard (1.5 km). On the northwest corner of this intersection is the fenced off Tuscany Community Association property. This is the corner where the temporary route joins the walk.

Temporary Bus Directions from Crowfoot Station to the temporary start of the walk: Catch bus # 74 Tuscany at stop 9879. Get off at stop 8432 on northbound Tuscany Springs Boulevard just north of Tuscany Boulevard. This stop is 9 minutes from Crowfoot Station. The bus frequency is 45 minutes daily. After getting off the bus walk back to the corner of Tuscany Boulevard and Tuscany Springs Boulevard. Turn right and walk west on Tuscany Boulevard to Tuscany Valley View. From here you follow the directions listed below until you reach the temporary bus stop at the end of the walk.

If you require better accessibility than the slope on the west side of Tuscany Valley View, stay on Tuscany Springs Boulevard. This road is still downhill but not quite as steep. When Tuscany Springs Boulevard ends at Tuscany Boulevard turn right and walk west to the next corner at Tuscany Valley View where you rejoin the route.

From the intersection of Tuscany Valley View and Tuscany Boulevard follow Tuscany Boulevard in a southwesterly direction. The next corner is the intersection with Tuscany Way. The aforementioned Tuscany Market is on the northwest corner. The route continues a few steps further southwest from the intersection along the south side of Tuscany Boulevard.

Look for a path beginning on the left behind the houses on Tuscany Village Court (1.9 km). This path has a gradual descent to where you pass St. Basil School on Tuscany Drive. St. Basil the Great who lived from 329 to

379 was the Archbishop of an area that is now in present day southeast Turkey. He was the founder of what was probably the first monastery in Asia Minor.

Cross Tuscany Drive (2.5 km) and continue ahead on Tuscany Glen Road to a T-intersection with Tuscany Glen Park (2.8 km). Cross the road and follow a path descending into a ravine. Note how the north facing slope on the left is heavily treed while the south facing slope on the right is much more open. When the route reaches a junction partway down the ravine take the path to the left and climb up the side of the ravine to reach Tuscany Estates Rise.

For better accessibility you can avoid the ravine by turning left on Tuscany Glen Park and then right onto Tuscany Estates Drive. Turn right onto Tuscany Estates Rise to reach the point where the path leads up out of the ravine.

Turn right at the end of the path leading up out of the ravine and follow Tuscany Estates Rise a few steps to where the road splits. You can go either left or right as this road makes a loop. At the far end of the loop, look for another path that leads to the top edge of the escarpment (3.8 km). This path turns left and passes behind the houses on Tuscany Estates Rise, Terrace and Point. For the next 5.5 km there are excellent views from the top of the escarpment.

The path will turn left at the south end of Tuscany Estates Point and head north. As the route nears the houses on Tuscany Estates Close, the path veers to the right and drops down a short descent and heads to the left to go uphill on the west side of Tuscany Hill. At the top of Tuscany Hill, Tuscany Estates Drive is on your left and Tuscany Meadows Drive is on the right (5.2 km).

To avoid the descent and ascent on Tuscany Hill turn left on a path leading to Tuscany Estates Close near the point where the path drops downhill towards Tuscany Hill. Follow Tuscany Estates Close to the left as it leads to Tuscany Estates Rise. Turn right on Tuscany Estates Rise and then turn right onto Tuscany Estates Drive. This road will lead you to the corner where the path finishes climbing up the west side of Tuscany Hill.

Cross to the Tuscany Meadows Drive side of the intersection to where there is a decorative entryway at the start of the path. This path heads southeast, passing behind the houses on Tuscany Meadows Crescent, Tuscany Ravine View and Mews. When the path turns to head east you will be behind the houses on Tuscany Ravine Close. The path then passes by the south end of Tuscany Ravine Point (6.2 km). Continue east on the path crossing through a large open space on the left with no houses.

The path turns left as it passes by the south end of the houses on Tuscany Ravine Road. At this point you begin to get excellent views east from the top of this escarpment on the west side of Twelve Mile Coulee. From the

Pathway near south end of Tuscany

path you can see Stoney Trail Bridge, Scenic Acres and the pedestrian tunnel under Stoney Trail. At the time of writing there is construction going on west of the tunnel for the new Stoney Trail and Nose Hill Drive interchange.

The path makes a sharp turn to the left and enters a section of the route with some descents and ascents behind the houses on Tuscany Ravine Heights. The view to the east is briefly blocked as you pass through this treed area. The path soon reaches a point with no houses on the left. This is the north end of the open space in the district. At the end of the open space the route will be behind the houses on Tuscany Ravine Terrace.

As the route heads north along the top edge of the escarpment overlooking Twelve Mile Coulee you will pass behind the houses on Tuscany Meadows Place and Tuscany Meadows Heights. The route will reach a rest area with a stone buffalo sculpture entitled *Sunning Buffalo* by Eric Peterson (8.6 km). This is the point where Tuscany Station Walk 1 – Twelve Mile Coulee descends and ascends the slope on the west side of the coulee. The two walks share a common route from the rest area north to Tuscany Boulevard. The path turns left behind the houses on Tuscany Hills Point and ends when you reach the intersection of Tuscany Boulevard and Tuscany Hills Road. This corner is the end of the temporary route. From there you catch a bus back to the Crowfoot Station.

Temporary Bus Directions from the end of the walk to Crowfoot
Station: When you reach the corner of Tuscany Boulevard and Tuscany Hills Road catch bus # 74 Tuscany at stop 8003 on eastbound Tuscany Boulevard. Get off the bus at stop 9879 back at Crowfoot Station. The scheduled time back to the station is 12 minutes. The bus frequency is 45 minutes daily.

Cross to the north side of Tuscany Boulevard and head north on Tuscany Valley View retracing your steps back to Tuscany Station (10.8 km).

Route Summary: (the temporary bus directions from Crowfoot Station are not included in this summary).

1. From the upper level of Tuscany Station turn left and cross the pedestrian overpass to the south side of Crowchild Trail.
2. Follow the access road to Tuscany Springs Boulevard.
3. Cross to the far side of the road and turn left.
4. At a path junction turn right and follow a path across a playing field.
5. At the next junction turn left and follow the path down the slope to Tuscany Valley View.
6. Turn left and follow the path south to Tuscany Boulevard. This is the corner where the temporary route from the bus stop joins this route.
7. Turn left and follow Tuscany Boulevard west crossing Tuscany Way.
8. After crossing Tuscany Way turn left on a path between houses.
9. Follow the path past St. Basil School to Tuscany Drive.
10. Cross Tuscany Drive and continue straight ahead on Tuscany Glen Road.
11. Cross Tuscany Glen Park and follow a path leading down into a ravine.
12. At a junction turn left climbing the slope to Tuscany Estates Rise.
13. Turn right and follow Tuscany Estates Rise either left or right to the far end of the loop.
14. Follow a path between houses and turn left on the path along the top of the escarpment.
15. As the route nears Tuscany Estates Close the path turns to the right and descends to the west side of Tuscany Hill.
16. Turn left and walk up Tuscany Hill to the intersection with Tuscany Estates Drive and Tuscany Meadows Drive.
17. Cross to the east side of Tuscany Hill and turn right on the path.
18. Follow the path south, east and then north until it ends at the intersection of Tuscany Boulevard and Tuscany Hills Road.
19. Cross to the north side of Tuscany Boulevard and head north on Tuscany Valley View retracing your earlier route back to Tuscany Station.

Tuscany Walk Three
Tuscany North

Walk Overview: This route follows paths and a trail through the north part of the community. The first and last 1.3 km is an out-and-back section connected to the loop portion of the route. Much of the loop passes through treed areas behind houses. The route also passes a pond where you may hear a chorus of frogs in the summer.

Length: 6.5 km

Route Description & Accessibility: On the out-and-back section of the route there is a fairly steep descent/ascent. An alternate route would add some extra distance to the walk and still involve hilly sections. After the first pond you follow a gradual uphill trail for about 400 m. Information on a detour for this trail is included in the text.

Food and Drink: There are no stores, coffee shops or restaurants along this route.

Washrooms: There are no public washrooms along this route.

Map References: Clear-View – A16, MapArt – 142
Rand McNally – 22, Sherlock – 7

Route Category: Walk – The route starts and ends at Tuscany Station (no bus is required).

The Walk: From the upper level of Tuscany Station turn left and cross the pedestrian overpass to the south side of Crowchild Trail. Follow the access road for the station parking lot to where it meets Tuscany Springs Boulevard.

Temporary Bus Directions from Crowfoot Station to the start of the walk: Catch bus # 74 Tuscany at stop 9879. Get off at the stop on northbound Tuscany Springs Boulevard close to Tuscarora Manor. This stop is 10 minutes from the station. The bus frequency is 45 minutes daily. This stop is close to where Tuscany Station parking lot will be located. From the stop follow the directions listed below until you reach the bus stop for the ride back to Crowfoot Station.

Cross to the far side of Tuscany Springs Boulevard and turn left on a path that heads south from the Sierras of Tuscany condos. At a junction turn right and follow a path west across a playing field to the top of a slope. At the next junction turn left following the path as it angles down the slope towards Tuscany Valley View (0.9 km).

If you require better accessibility than the path down the slope you will need to turn right from the station access road onto Tuscany Springs Boulevard and then turn left on Tuscany Valley View. The topography of the community can make it difficult to find a relatively flat route with good accessibility.

When you reach Tuscany Valley View turn left and follow the path south to the first intersection at Tuscany Drive. Cross to the west side of Tuscany Valley View and turn right, walking past a small ornamental area to where a path heads west behind the houses on the north side of Tuscany Drive. There is a large open field north of the path. On the left behind the houses is a stream. At times the water can be quite high. In the winter the ice builds up along the streambed.

The path turns right and heads north following the edge of the stream. The houses on the left on Tuscany Valley Green face towards the path. The route passes a small bridge crossing the stream to that road. When the route reaches a path junction stay left as the path turns northwesterly and crosses the stream. Just before the path again turns north you pass an area on the right where the base of the trees and bushes are under water during certain times of the year. On the left as you turn right and head north is the frog chorus pond.

After a couple of steps the route reaches a junction overlooking the pond where a trail leads to the left past the north side of the pond (1.6 km). This

Trees in the water

junction is the end of the out-and-back section of this route. Turn left onto the trail to begin the loop portion of the walk. The trail goes west and turns north on a gradual ascent behind the houses on the right on Tuscany Springs Terrace. The trail ends at Tuscany Springs Hill (1.9 km).

To avoid this path go right from the junction to Tusslewood Drive. Turn left and walk northwest to Tuscany Springs Hill. Turn left walking southwest to where the trail ends on the left and a path starts on the right. At this point you rejoin the route.

From the end of the trail on Tuscany Springs Hill, cross this road and follow a paved path leading into a more treed area with the houses of Tuscany Reserve Gate on the left and the houses of Tusslewood Heights on the right. The path reaches a junction on the edge of an open space with a playground. Turn right between the houses and cross Tusslewood Heights (2.2 km). The path resumes on the far side of the road. The route now heads north with the houses of Tusslewood Heights on both sides. This treed area behind the houses is very pleasant.

The route turns slightly to the left and begins heading northwesterly with the houses of Tusslewood Drive on the right and the houses of Tuscany

Deer sculpture on Tusslewood Drive

Reserve Rise on the left. The path then turns left and ends at Tuscany Reserve Rise (2.8 km). Turn right and walk a few steps north to Tusslewood Drive. Cross Tusslewood Drive and follow a wider path between houses to Tuscany Summit Terrace.

Turn right and walk a few steps to the postal boxes located on the north side of Tuscany Summit Terrace. Turn left and follow a path heading north (3.1 km). The path makes a loop to the right passing a playground and ending at Tuscany Springs Boulevard (3.5 km). Near the top of the loop there is a junction where you turn right. Near this junction there is a pipe where the water that flows through Tuscany passes under Crowchild Trail as it enters Tuscany.

Make a slight detour to the right when you reach Tuscany Springs Boulevard and then turn left onto Tusslewood Drive. Just a few steps along this road (3.7 km), there is a sculpture of a deer that has been placed so it appears to be just leaving the treed area behind the sculpture. The sculpture is by Don & Shirley Begg. From here retrace your steps back to Tuscany Springs Boulevard.

Walk a few steps northeast on Tuscany Springs Boulevard and turn right onto a path leading in a southeasterly direction. This treed area is much wider than the areas you passed through earlier. On the left are the houses on Tuscany Springs Boulevard. Beyond the trees on the right are the houses on Tusslewood Drive. At certain times of the year the water in the area around the trees on the right often covers the base of the trees. Stay on the main path ignoring any paths leading left or right to the nearby streets. Just before the path reaches Tusslewood Drive you pass a small pond on the left. A gravel path on the west side of this pond leads to where you can see another small pond. Cross Tusslewood Drive and walk a few steps south to reach the junction overlooking the frog chorus pond (4.9 km). Stay on the paved path and retrace your earlier route back to Tuscany Station (6.5 km).

Temporary Bus Directions to Crowfoot Station from the end of the walk: When you reach the corner of Tuscany Valley View and Tuscany Drive catch bus # 74 Tuscany at stop 3852 back to stop 9879 at Crowfoot Station. The scheduled time back to Crowfoot Station is 13 minutes. The bus frequency is 45 minutes daily.

Route Summary: (the temporary bus directions from Crowfoot Station are not included in this summary).

1. From the upper level of Tuscany Station turn left and cross the pedestrian overpass to the south side of Crowchild Trail.
2. Follow the access road to Tuscany Springs Boulevard.
3. Cross to the far side of the road and turn left.
4. At a path junction turn right and follow a path across a playing field.

5. At the next junction turn left and follow the path down the slope to Tuscany Valley View.
6. Turn left and follow the path south to the intersection with Tuscany Drive.
7. Cross to the west side of the road and turn right and then left on a path behind the houses on the north side of Tuscany Drive.
8. The path turns right and heads north.
9. At a junction by a small bridge take the right branch.
10. At the next junction turn left.
11. At a junction overlooking a pond turn left on a gravel trail.
12. When the trail ends at Tuscany Springs Hill cross to the far side of the road and follow a path into a treed area.
13. At a junction near an open area turn right and follow the path to Tusslewood Heights.
14. Cross the road and continue on the path.
15. The path ends at Tuscany Reserve Rise.
16. Turn right and walk north to Tusslewood Drive.
17. Cross the road and follow a wider path between houses to Tuscany Summit Terrace.
18. Turn right and then by the postal boxes turn left on a path.
19. The path makes a loop and ends at Tuscany Springs Boulevard.
20. Turn right and then left on Tusslewood Drive to view a sculpture.
21. Retrace your steps back to Tuscany Springs Boulevard.
22. Walk a few steps north on Tuscany Springs Boulevard and turn right on a path leading into a treed area.
23. Follow the path until it reaches Tusslewood Drive.
24. Cross the road and walk a few steps on the path to reach the junction with the gravel trail.
25. From here retrace your route back to Tuscany Station.

Tuscany Walk Four
Royal Oak

Walk Overview: This route passes two small ponds before descending into a ravine past a third pond. The route then makes a circuit around a wetlands area. Watch for birds or muskrats at the wetlands. The section of the route through the ravine is a bit isolated so use your own discretion about walking alone.

Length: 5.3 km

Route Description & Accessibility: This loop route has poor accessibility.

The walking surface is a mix of sidewalks, paved path and trails. From Tuscany Station there is a gradual ascent north on Rocky Ridge Road to a path. This path then ends abruptly and you follow a very rough trail before the path starts again. The route then descends a steep trail to reach the bottom of the ravine. The trail in the ravine can be wet and muddy. At the wetlands part of the loop the route crosses some large rocks and follows a rough trail. No alternate route for these sections is included in the text.

Food and Drink: There are no food stores or restaurants along this route.

Washrooms: There are no public washrooms along the route.

Map References: Clear-View – 1, MapArt – 143
Rand McNally – 11, Sherlock – 7 & 8

Route Category: Walk – The route starts and ends at Tuscany Station (no bus is required).

The Walk: From the upper level of Tuscany Station cross the pedestrian overpass to the north side of Crowchild Trail and walk through the parking north to the south end of Rocky Ridge Road.

Temporary Bus Directions from Crowfoot Station to the start of the walk: Catch bus # 158 Royal Oak at stop 9878. Get off at

Pond at the west end of Royal Birch Boulevard

Coots at Royal Oak Drive Wetlands

stop 8901 close to Rocky Ridge Road and Rocky Vista Drive. The stop is 14 minutes from Crowfoot Station. The bus frequency is 30 minutes daily. From here you follow the directions listed below until the route reaches the bus stop where you ride back to Crowfoot Station.

Walk north on Rocky Ridge Road past the new Calgary Temple of the Church of Jesus Christ of Latter-Day Saints on the right north of Royal Oak Drive. Rocky Ridge Road has a gradual ascent. After passing Royal Elm Road and just before Royal Highland Road a path starts on your right (1.2 km). The path goes by the north side of a pond where you may see waterfowl. On the left along this section of path is a high retaining wall behind the houses on Royal Highland Court.

Near the northeast corner of the pond the path splits. The right path soon ends. Follow the left path crossing over Royal Abbey Rise and continuing on the path (1.5 km). At the next junction the left branch leads to Royal Birkdale Crescent. Take the right branch as it goes past the houses on Royal Birkdale Crescent. On the right is the ravine you will wander through shortly.

The path soon ends as you turn left and follow a rather rough trail along the top of the slope above the ravine (1.9 km). Continue on this trail until it joins another path near a second pond. This pond is near the west end of Royal Birch Boulevard (2.1 km). You may also spot waterfowl here. Retrace your steps a short distance and turn left following a trail down into the ravine

(2.4 km). The trail in this section of the ravine can be muddy and wet. Turn left and follow the trail until you reach the end of a path near a small pond. Follow this path south passing a playground just before Royal Oak Drive.

Turn left and walk to the corner at 100 Royal Crest Bay and cross to the south side of Royal Oak Drive. Turn right and walk west to the ornamental gateway where you turn left at the Royal Oak Drive Wetlands (2.9 km). There are several ponds in the wetlands. A paved path leads to the right along the north side of the largest pond. Dirt trails extend along the edge of the other ponds. A gazebo-like structure with benches provides a nice rest area to sit and watch for birds.

Turn left before you reach the gazebo and watch your step crossing an area with large rocks. On the other side of the rocks, angle to the left and follow a trail beside the wetlands. Watch for birds as you stroll the trail. On one visit here, three muskrats were spotted. On the left beyond an old wire fence is another wetlands area. At the far end of the wetlands, turn to the right and walk towards the paved path. Walk back along the path past the gazebo and through the ornamental gateway to return to Royal Oak Drive.

Temporary Bus Directions from the end of the route back to Crowfoot Station: Catch bus # 158 Royal Oak at stop 8895 on eastbound Royal Oak Drive near Royal Terrace. Get off at stop 9878 back at Crowfoot Station. The scheduled time back to Crowfoot Station is 14 minutes. The bus frequency is 30 minutes daily.

Turn left and walk west along Royal Oak Drive back to Rocky Ridge Road. Make a left turn and retrace your steps back to Tuscany Station (5.3 km).

Route Summary: (the temporary bus directions from Crowfoot Station are not included in this summary).
1. From the upper level of Tuscany Station turn right and cross the pedestrian overpass to the north side of Crowchild Trail.
2. Walk through the parking area to the south end of Rocky Ridge Road.
3. Walk north on Rocky Ridge Road.
4. Just before Royal Highland Road turn right onto a path.
5. At a path junction turn left and cross Royal Abbey Rise, continuing on the path.
6. At the next junction take the right branch.
7. When the path ends follow a trail along the top edge of the ravine.
8. The trail joins another path overlooking a pond.
9. Retrace your steps a short distance on the trail and follow a trail to the left descending the slope into the ravine.
10. Turn left and follow the trail through the ravine until you reach the end of a path near a pond.
11. Follow this path to Royal Oak Drive.
12. Turn left and walk to the corner at 100 Royal Crest Bay and cross to the south side of Royal Oak Drive.

13. Turn right and walk west to the ornamental gateway where you turn left at the Royal Oak Drive Wetlands.
13. Turn left and use caution stepping across some large rocks to reach a trail on the far side of the wetlands.
14. At the far end of the wetlands turn right on the trail until it joins the path on the other side of the wetlands.
15. Turn right and follow this path back to the gateway on Royal Oak Drive. This is the end of the temporary route.
16. Turn left and follow Royal Oak Drive west to Rocky Ridge Road.
17. Turn left and retrace your steps back to Tuscany Station.

Bibliography

Atkin, John. *Sky Train Explorer*. Vancouver: Steller Press, 2005.

Beattie, Lori. *Calgary's Best Hikes and Walks*. Calgary: Fifth House Ltd., 2002.

Bullick, Terry. *Calgary Parks and Pathways – A City's Treasures*. Calgary: Blue Couch Books, 2007.

Foley, Jim. *Calgary's Natural Parks – Yours to Explore*. Calgary: Calgary Field Naturalists' Society, 2006.

Humber, Donna Mae. *What's In A Name ... Calgary?* Calgary: Detselig Enterprises Ltd., 1994.

Humber, Donna Mae. *What's In A Name ... Calgary? Volume 2*. Calgary: Detselig Enterprises Ltd., 1995.

Kwasny, Barbara., Peake, Elaine. *A Second Look at Calgary's Public Art*. Calgary: Detselig Enterprises Ltd., 1992.

Sanders, Harry. *Historic Walks of Calgary*. Calgary: Red Deer Press, 2005.

Walks by distance

3 km or shorter
2.1 km – Sunnyside Walk 4 – Gladstone Road & Kensington Road
2.1 km – Dalhousie Walk 8 – Hamptons
2.3 km – University Walk 1 – Campus – Short Loop
2.6 km – Sunnyside Walk 2 – Sunnyside – Short Loop
3.0 km – Lions Park Walk 3 – Lions Park & Hounsfield Heights

3.1 to 5 km
3.2 km – Dalhousie Walk 2 – Edgemont, Hawkwood & Ranchlands
3.3 km – Sunnyside Walk 6 – Nose Hill Park (Rubbing Stone Hill)
3.5 km – Sunnyside Walk 1 – Sunnyside – Long Loop
3.7 km – Sunnyside Walk 3 – Riley Park & Westmount Boulevard
3.7 km – Brentwood Walk 1 – Research Park & Varsity Acres
3.7 km – Dalhousie Walk 3 – Edgemont Escarpment
4.5 km – University Walk 2 – Campus – Long Loop

5.1 to 7 km
5.2 km – Lions Park Walk 1 – Briar Hill, St. Andrews Heights
　　　　& Shagnessey Heights Park
5.2 km – Brentwood Walk 3 – Brentwood Murals
5.3 km – Tuscany Walk 4 – Royal Oak
5.6 km – Banff Trail Walk 2 – University Heights & West Campus Pond
5.7 km – Lions Park Walk 2 – Bow River Pathway - 29th Street to Shouldice
　　　　Park
5.7 km – Dalhousie Walk 7 – Hidden Valley
6.0 km – Dalhousie Walk 6 – Nose Hill Park (Meadowlark Prairie)
6.1 km – Sunnyside Walk 5 – Bow River Pathway & West Hillhurst
6.4 km – Dalhousie Walk 1 – Edgemont Ravines to Dalhousie Station
6.4 km – Crowfoot Walk 1 – Citadel to Crowfoot Station
6.4 km – Crowfoot Walk 5 – Scenic Acres
6.5 km – Tuscany Walk 3 – Tuscany North
6.6 km – SAIT/ACAD/Jubilee Walk 2 – Capitol Hill & Mount Pleasant
6.8 km – Brentwood Walk 2 – Nose Hill Park (Many Owls Valley)
　　　　& Whispering Woods
6.9 km – Banff Trail Walk 1 – Banff Trail, Canmore Park & Collingwood

7.1 km or longer
7.4 km – SAIT/ACAD/Jubilee Walk 1 – Confederation Park
7.6 km – Tuscany Walk 1 – Twelve Mile Coulee
7.7 km – Crowfoot Walk 4 – Bow Crescent & Bowness Road
7.9 km – SAIT/ACAD/Jubilee Walk 3 – Rosedale & Crescent Heights
8.7 km – Crowfoot 3 – West Bowness & Valley Ridge Escarpment
8.8 km – Dalhousie Walk 5 – Bowmont Park East
9.1 km – Dalhousie Walk 4 – Bowmont Park (Waterfall Valley)
9.5 km – Crowfoot Walk 2 – Bowmont Park West, Baker Park
      & Bowness Park
10.8 km – Tuscany Walk 2 – Tuscany Escarpment

Walks by Category

Walk – Walk starts and ends at station (no bus is required)
Sunnyside Walk 1 – Sunnyside – Long Loop
Sunnyside Walk 2 – Sunnyside – Short Loop
Sunnyside Walk 3 – Riley Park & Westmount Boulevard
Sunnyside Walk 4 – Gladstone Road & Kensington Road
Sunnyside Walk 5 – Bow River Pathway & West Hillhurst
SAIT/ACAD/Jubilee Walk 1 – Confederation Park
SAIT/ACAD/Jubilee Walk 2 – Capitol Hill & Mount Pleasant
SAIT/ACAD/Jubilee Walk 3 – Rosedale & Crescent Heights
Lions Park Walk 1 – Briar Hill, St. Andrews Heights & Shagnessey Heights
      Park
Lions Park Walk 3 – Lions Park & Hounsfield Heights
Banff Trail Walk 1 – Banff Trail, Canmore Park & Collingwood
Banff Trail Walk 2 – University Heights & West Campus Pond
University Walk 1 – Campus – Short loop
University Walk 2 – Campus – Long loop
Brentwood Walk 1 – Research Park & Varsity Acres
Brentwood Walk 3 – Brentwood Murals
Dalhousie Walk 4 – Bowmont Park (Waterfall Valley)
Dalhousie Walk 5 – Bowmont Park East
Crowfoot Walk 5 – Scenic Acres
Tuscany Walk 1 – Twelve Mile Coulee
Tuscany Walk 2 – Tuscany Escarpment

Tuscany Walk 3 – Tuscany North
Tuscany Walk 4 – Royal Oak

Bus/Walk – Ride bus to start of route and walk back to station (showing minutes by bus from station to start of route)
Dalhousie Walk 1 – Edgemont Ravines to Dalhousie Station
Crowfoot Walk 1 – Citadel to Crowfoot Station

Walk/Bus – Walk to end of route and ride bus back to station (showing minutes by bus from end of route to station)
Crowfoot Walk 2 – Bowmont Park West, Baker Park & Bowness Park

Bus/Walk/Bus – Ride bus to start of route and ride bus back to station from end of route (showing minutes by bus to start of route and by bus from end of route to station)
Sunnyside Walk 6 – Nose Hill Park (Rubbing Stone Hill)
Lions Park Walk 2 – Bow River Pathway – 29th Street to Shouldice Park
Brentwood Walk 2 – Nose Hill Park (Many Owls Valley) & Whispering Woods
Dalhousie Walk 2 – Edgemont, Hawkwood & Ranchlands
Dalhousie Walk 3 – Edgemont Escarpment
Dalhousie Walk 6 – Nose Hill Park (Meadowlark Prairie)
Dalhousie Walk 7 – Hidden Valley
Dalhousie Walk 8 – Hamptons
Crowfoot Walk 3 – West Bowness & Valley Ridge Escarpment
Crowfoot Walk 4 – Bow Crescent & Bowness Road

Also by Peyto Lake Books

Walking Guidebooks
Walk Calgary's Escarpments & Bluffs (2005), $16.95
Calgary LRT Walks: The South Stations (2013) $19.00

Calgary Parks
Discover North Calgary's Parks and Green Spaces (2006), $13.95
Discover Southeast Calgary's Parks and Green Spaces (2007), $12.95
Discover Southwest Calgary's Parks and Green Spaces (2008), $19.95

Banff Town Warden Journals
Banff Town Warden – 1914 to 1922 (2002), $19.95
Banff Town Warden 2 – 1923 to 1928 (2004), $19.95
Banff Town Warden 3 – 1929 to 1934 (2008), $19.95
Banff Town Warden 4 – 1935 to 1941 (2009), $19.95

Trivia Guides
Bill Peyto Guide to Canadian Rockies Trivia Volume 1 (2003), $10
Bill Peyto Guide to Canadian Rockies Trivia Volume 2 (2003), $10

Upcoming Publications
The author is currently working on Calgary LRT Walks: The Northeast Stations and Calgary LRT Walks: The Downtown and West Stations.

About the Author

David Peyto (Pea-toe) is a retired elementary school physical education teacher with an interest in walking and history. Throughout his teaching career he organized and lead walks for the students, fellow teachers and parent volunteers. He is planning additional walking guidebooks. David and his wife Linda live in Calgary.

Northwest Stations

Hillhurst United Church

West gate in Riley Park

Confederation Park

Balmoral School

Bow River in Bowmont Park

Edgemont Ravine Pond

Baker Park

Old sidewalk in Baker Park